The Weaving

A Journey to *Corrie ten Boom Live*

Evelyn Hinds

MW01204704

The Weaving

Copyright ©2007 Evelyn Hinds. All rights reserved.

No part of this book may be reproduced in any form without written permission in advance from the publisher. International rights and foreign translations available only through negotiation with CornerStone Leadership Institute.

Inquiries regarding permission for use of the material contained in this book should be addressed to:

CornerStone Leadership Institute
P.O. Box 764087
Dallas, TX 75376
888.789.LEAD

Printed in the United States of America
ISBN: 0-9788137-3-1

Credits
Design, art direction, and production   Melissa Monogue, Back Porch Creative, Plano, TX
info@BackPorchCreative.com

Table of Contents

The Weaving

Preface

For I know the plans that I have for you, declares the Lord, plans for welfare and not for calamity to give you a future and a hope.

Jeremiah 29:11 NIV

I remember the first time I really read that verse back in the early 1980s. It sounded a little too good to be true. My life was in turmoil, and I was struggling on all fronts. My relationship, my work, my son's health, and my emotions were out of control. I was depressed and angry.

My friend Laura made a drawing of calligraphy art of the verse from Jeremiah and sent it to me. I framed it and hung it on the wall. I hoped it would sink in and that most of all that it was true. I tried to believe it as best as I could. I cried a lot, and I prayed.

Then you will call upon me and come and pray to Me, and I will listen to you. And you will seek Me and find Me, when you search for Me with all your heart.

Jeremiah 29:12-13 NIV

The following chapters tell the story of my journey to finding God. Today I have a ministry portraying a beloved Christian speaker and author of a generation ago, Corrie ten Boom.

In my travels performing my one-woman dramatic presentation, I meet many of Corrie's fans who have been deeply touched by her books and speaking. However, I find that I introduce her story to many more children and adults who have never heard of her. So for those who missed her story while she was alive and for those born since her death, I include a few words of factual introduction.

Corrie ten Boom (1892-1983) was a Dutch woman who survived the Holocaust and an infamous Nazi death camp, Ravensbruck. She was a Christian who was imprisoned for hiding and protecting Jews in Holland during Hitler's reign. Corrie earned Israel's designation as a "Righteous Gentile." She committed her life after the end of the war to traveling around the world telling her story and preaching the gospel. Corrie would boldly proclaim, "God has no problems with our lives, only plans!" The fact that she had been a prisoner in a concentration camp during World War II became the reason so many people listened to her share her faith.

After the war, Corrie wrote over twenty books describing her experiences and how God had prepared her for her work. Her story was made into a movie in 1975 by the Billy Graham organization, World Wide Pictures. She became a beloved speaker over the years, and left a legacy in audio tapes as well as print and film.

Corrie endured unimaginable suffering at the hands of the Nazis. However, by a clerical error, she was miraculously released from the concentration camp and returned to Holland a few months before the end of the war. In those dark days, she began to write her first book. In *A Prisoner and Yet,* she described a moment in her journey of faith in God:

> I went with Betsie to the barracks, and a bit later was lying beside her in bed. I did not sleep, but rested quietly—and there was peace in my heart. God makes no mistakes. Everything looks like a confused piece of embroidery work, meaningless and ugly. But that is the underside. Some day we shall see the right side and shall be amazed and thankful.

In her worldwide ministry, Corrie used a piece of embroidery to illustrate the Bible's message that God has a plan for our lives. We often see our lives as a mess, but that is the underside. God sees the victory because his view is the beautifully completed plan. Corrie later found and used a poem, *The Weaving,* in her ministry that described that message.

In her book *In My Father's House,* Corrie wrote about how God had prepared her from childhood for her ministry in the concentration camp and afterwards. That book encouraged me to look at my own life. Was I bold enough to believe in and apply that principle? I asked myself and God, "Can anything be made from this mess of my life? Is there a plan for me?" My eyes of faith compelled me to respond with "Yes!" I challenge my audiences and readers to look at the principle and examine their lives for evidence of God's hand.

Today, I am the founder of Arts Touching Hearts, Inc., a non-profit ministry committed to sharing the message of God through the arts. I am often asked how I got started with my work. In attempting to answer that question, I had to dig deep into my past. I began to see my story in view of God's weaving a plan for me before I knew it.

This book is my tribute to the courageous woman whose testimony has been life-changing for me. Ultimately, this book is my tribute to an all-powerful God who has woven my life for his plans and purposes. It is my hope that Corrie's story and my story will encourage you to ask for the eyes of faith to believe that God has a plan for you!

Evelyn Hinds
Valley Ranch, Texas
November 18, 2006

The Poem and the Principle

My *Corrie ten Boom Live* performance begins with a poem that Corrie used to illustrate the stories of her life that took her from Holland to a German concentration camp and around the world with the message, "God has no problems with our lives, only plans!"

The Weaving

*My life is like a weaving
Between my God and me
I do not choose the colors
He worketh steadily.
Sometimes He weaveth sorrow
And I in foolish pride
Forget He sees the upper
And I the underside.
Not till the loom is silent
And the shuttles cease to fly
Will God unroll the canvas
And explain the reason why.
The dark threads are as needful
In the skillful Weaver's hand
As the threads of gold and silver
In the pattern He has planned.*

Unknown

The Weaving

My First Performance of *Corrie ten Boom Live*

The church auditorium was filled with ladies seated around tables. Our large sanctuary had been reconfigured and decorated for the ladies' retreat. It was dark except for the spotlights on the stage. The voices of the women were quieted to a hush. I walked slowly, but with a deliberate stride, from my chair at the back of the platform up to the podium, dressed in the 1950s-era Corrie ten Boom costume I had put together. I was carrying books, a notebook, and a vintage purse. I settled my things on top of the wooden podium. I made a bit of dramatic ceremony of pulling out an embroidery piece, a hanky, and a glove from the long-out-of-style patent leather purse. I had stuffed them in the purse to use for visual aids.

"Gud evening. I bring you greetings from Holland," I began my one-woman dramatization as Corrie ten Boom. I recited *The Weaving* poem using the embroidery piece. After the poem I began to tell Corrie's story. I could hear her voice in my head, as I used her choices of words and accent as faithfully as I could. I got goosebumps when I thundered out one of her well known lines, "Der is no pit so deep dat da love of God is not deeper still!"

I was nervous, but surprised myself with the boldness in my voice. Thoughts in my mind raised familiar doubts. *What were you thinking? What are you doing up here on stage? Haven't you volunteered for enough other things?* Even with those thoughts running through my head, I came alive as Corrie. From deep in my heart I was awakened to a sense that this was part of my purpose on earth. My dramatic presentation that began that night would begin to change my life in ways I could not imagine.

Corrie began to tell her story as she might have when she was alive. I wanted to be as faithful as I could to Corrie's own words. I also knew I had to give my audience a little more history than she would have needed to do in her days after World War II. Books and tapes of her messages played over and over in my mind, as I tried to communicate the nuggets of Corrie's life and faith with a Dutch accent, and the demeanor and purpose of an old woman on a mission. My mind raced as I wondered if I could remember and deliver the lines I had planned.

"I am too old for prison life, but for me it would be an honor to give my life for God's chosen people," *Corrie* quoted her 84-year-old father. That was his response when his friends warned him of the danger he was in for helping the Jews. After a pause *Corrie* continued, "For you see, that is what he did."

I had read that Corrie's grandfather had a love for the Jewish people that began when he read and accepted the Biblical command to pray for the peace of Jerusalem. His belief motivated him to start a prayer group for the Jewish people in 1844. That decision had shaped the family. It was passed as a legacy to Corrie's father and to his family.

Father ten Boom had such a strong faith in God that he was willing to die for the Jews! I got goosebumps again, as I got a fresh realization of his conviction. As those words went out to my audience in that darkened room, they washed over me in a fresh filling of the Spirit. I wept. I prayed, God, have you so transformed me that I could be used to communicate your work in the Ten Booms? Partly I wept over Father ten Boom's conviction and partly over my awe that God would use me as a vessel.

I wiped my very real tears with the vintage hanky I carried. I continued on with the stories, weeping as my emotions moved me. Although I knew many of the women in my audience, I could not see anyone's face in the darkness. I wondered if they were getting the message. Even though I had the warm feeling of being connected with other souls, I knew these feelings were not proof.

Stories from Corrie's books and tapes were the foundation for my performance. I had edited them down to what were the most powerful ones to me. I had an outline written down that had emerged from the logical sequence in my mind. In the rush of adrenaline mixed with nervousness, I never even glanced at it. It was truly a spontaneous performance. I wrapped up my presentation and gathered the books with the slow but deliberate motions of an old woman. My heart sank as I saw the glove I had forgotten to explain to the audience. I had missed my chance. I thought, *Oh well, it is too late now. The show must go on.*

As Corrie, I carefully descended the few carpeted steps to a chair reserved for me at one of the front tables. The pastor's wife closed the evening with prayer and an invitation to counsel any woman who wanted to come forward. I lined up with other leaders to be available to counsel.

A line formed for me, but I soon realized it was not for me at all—but for Corrie. The women came for a hug. It was the greeting that churchwomen in Claremore, Oklahoma were comfortable with to express their love. I noticed that the cheeks that touched mine were wet. There must have been weeping in the darkness at their tables. My heart exploded with joy when I realized that Corrie had touched their hearts just as she had mine.

Some women asked for my autograph. My racing mind was trying to make sense of that request. *An autograph?* Then I realized that my performance was so convincing, they thought I *was* Corrie. It was 1997. Didn't they realize that Corrie had died in 1983? Unable to find the words to explain, I simply signed "Evelyn Hinds as Corrie ten Boom."

In my mind I heard Corrie's voice from one of her tapes encourage me, "Ask God to use you, and I tell you he will use you." I knew that request was the desire of my heart for many years, but another voice often spoke in my mind too. *You've always been a square peg trying to fit in a round hole. How could God use you?* I recognized that as the voice of the enemy sending thoughts to discourage me. Refusing to listen to that voice, I held on to my belief in Corrie's message that "God has no problems with our lives, only plans."

I wondered what God was up to in my life. I shot up a quick prayer, "I like doing this, but only if you want me to do it." I was excited to see what would happen next. I sensed this was a dramatic and pivotal turn in my life.

Over the days and years since that evening, I have thought long and hard about my past and looked for God's hand. What made me able to connect so deeply with Corrie ten Boom? What were the significant threads in the weaving of my life that prepared me for this dramatic turn in my life? I often felt like I didn't fit in, and found myself walking a solitary path. Interestingly, moments of solitude were one of my connecting threads with Corrie's story.

The Weaving

Weaving in Solitary

It was Christmas day in 1968 when I left my family in Kansas City, and boarded an airplane bound for New York City. Lyrics from Peter, Paul, and Mary's current hit song, "Leaving on a Jet Plane," played in my head—"Don't know when I'll be back again."

I dropped out of the University of Kansas, and scrapped my plans to pursue teaching. Dropping out was not unusual back then. I was a nineteen-year-old "child of the '60s," and dropping out was in the air. I decided to marry my boyfriend, packed two suitcases, and set out for a new life.

My boyfriend was a born-and-bred New Yorker. He was older than me and seemed to have life figured out. I thought I did, but I hit a snag in the form of a health problem that sent me into a deep, dark depression. A moment of clarity was pivotal in my decision to marry and move away. It came when I was in a hospital bed suffering through unsuccessful medical care. Tears burned my cheeks as I despaired of life. Through those tears, a belief crystallized deep down in my heart—*Life is not about stuff, it's about people.*

Marriage seemed like the only decision I could make. John proposed, and I decided to go ahead and give it a try. I was also trying to get as far away as I could from my Midwest upbringing. I set out to begin a new life in an apartment in Queens. I hoped to become a different and happier person.

I expected to live in New York for the rest of my life. I had no reason to believe that my husband would ever consider moving out of "The Big Apple," and I wanted to get away from home. Many things did not work out like I thought—and living in New York was only one of them, although I did learn something about loneliness in the year and a half that I lived there. That loneliness was part of what I drew upon when I read and studied about Corrie ten Boom's loneliness in prison.

Corrie summed up her months of solitary confinement with two words, "Terrible suffering!" She did not strike me as one to belabor her suffering. In fact, I sensed her description was a great understatement. My mind visualized Corrie's cell that was only a few paces wide. I empathized as she recalled being so terribly alone. She had spent her then fifty-two years surrounded by her loving family, and suddenly she was utterly alone. Corrie described that she sometimes stood with her back to the wall, spreading her hands out and pressing against the wall—as if she were trying to hold it back from closing in on her. I almost choked, thinking of the claustrophobia she must have felt.

The filth Corrie described in her cell sickened me. My nose burned as I imagined the smells that seemed even worse than the sights. There was the blanket that had been vomited on by a prisoner before her. The mattress was not only hard, but had the stench of fermented hay. The bucket for her toilet facility was always present. I wondered how much a human being could stand. Solitary confinement tested Corrie's endurance, but also taught her some of her greatest lessons.

Corrie believed in the power of praise to lift her spirits, so she began to sing in her lonely cell. When the guards heard her, she was told to shut up or be put in a dark cell where the prisoner had to stand in cold water. I felt her outrage that she would not be able to use her voice to comfort herself.

Corrie loved to talk, and she was accustomed to commanding attention. With no one around she found herself making friends with the ants that crawled on the floor. I tried to imagine being lonely enough to consider the companionship of an ant.

Before her imprisonment, Corrie had never really been alone. She was the youngest of the children in a family known for their hospitality. The family home, the Beje, was always filled with activity when Corrie had lived there. She taught many classes, and led a group of Dutch underground workers during the war. Corrie had a history of being surrounded with people.

When I read and reflected on Corrie's solitary confinement story, I flashed back to the long afternoons and evenings when I was alone in my New York apartment. That was the first time in my life that I was away from my chaotic family life or frenzied college dorm life. I knew no one except my husband and his friends and family. They eyed me with distrust and referred to me as "the girl from Kansas." It did no good to try to explain to these lifelong New Yorkers that Kansas City was in Missouri. I gave up trying; I felt misunderstood.

I was alone and trying to be grown up. I rarely went out, unless my husband went with me.

When my husband was at work, I spent my time alone comforting myself with reading and sewing. The loneliness I felt gave me a glimpse of Corrie's pain. I was not in a cell, but sometimes my apartment felt like a prison. The dangers of going out alone in New York City held me as a prisoner of fear. I wanted to have someone to talk to, but I did not know anyone that spoke my language. I enjoyed intellectually stimulating conversation. I had been named "heavy Evy" by a college friend because I was so "deep." Didn't I have the vague hope that the world would become deeper and more thoughtful because of the revolution of the '60s? I was a thinker, and my world had shrunk because all the people I knew lived halfway across the country. I was learning that the New Yorkers I knew did not think or speak the way I did.

Letters from my busy, sweet mother were a treat back then. Mama had seven of us kids to tend to, in addition to our Dad. I was the first to leave home to marry. My youngest sister was only a toddler, and I knew Mama had little time for writing. I also knew she felt inadequate about writing because she only had an eighth grade education—plus Mama was neither a reader nor a writer. I knew it was an act of love to take the time to write to me. She wrote about my siblings and the weather and the activities at home.

One day I received a letter from Mama with a poem she had clipped from something. It described life as a weaving of God. It struck me as odd that Mama would include it with her letter since she really was not one to appreciate poetry. I read and reread it, and tried to understand why it had impressed her enough to send it to me. I figured she was probably trying to teach me something about God that I did not want to hear. In my mind, I felt like I was old enough and sophisticated enough to have my own opinions about God. I did not welcome any more parenting about religion.

A line from the poem stuck in my head—"The shuttles cease to fly." I wondered if that meant death. I was not even sure what shuttles were, but it seemed sad, and I did not want any more sadness in my life. I forgot all about it.

Nearly thirty years later and many miles away from my New York experiences, I was in Oklahoma reciting *The Weaving*, the poem Corrie used about God as the weaver of our lives. In film footage, I watched Corrie recite the poem and hold up handwork where the top said "Jesus is Victor" and the underneath was a tangled mess of threads. I created an embroidered piece similar to the one she used, and I used it and the poem to begin my dramatization as Corrie did to illustrate her message.

It was not hard for me to see how Corrie's life illustrated the poem's encouraging message. Her experiences in the concentration camp gave her an audience. She declared, "Even though we was prisoners, we experienced so much of da love of God." She touched people's hearts around the world when she spoke, and used her stories of suffering and God's faithfulness to her to encourage others. At my performances, the story of Corrie's life and the poem continues to touch people's hearts.

As I recited the poem to a friend in my Oklahoma kitchen and explained a little bit of the theology behind it, I had another startling moment of clarity. The poem Corrie ten Boom used to touch others, the poem I used in my performances and quoted to friends, was the same poem that had touched my mother!

The Weaving was used by many people. Corrie said she found it when she came to America to illustrate the message that she and her sister discussed in prison. Betsie encouraged Corrie, "Everything that happens to us is a preparation for the work we will do next."

That moment in my kitchen I realized that God was working out His plan for me—even before I was able to realize it. During my loneliness in New York which was often like a prison, I had no idea that God was at work on his plan for me. I had no idea that I would learn and recite the poem I rejected from my mother years ago. I was flooded with hope that God had been preparing me all along!

Looking back at my life, I realized that God had to prepare me to trust him. My natural independence had to be broken. My brokenness came as a dark time of tears.

Tears

My heart was broken and tears were silently streaming down my face. I was embarrassed because I was at work and in front of the public. This day I had been assigned the reception desk and I was the first face people encountered when they walked in the door. I tried to stop crying, but the tears kept coming.

I was crying because I had just heard unimaginable, heartbreaking news. My not-yet-four-year-old son had been diagnosed with a serious medical problem. I did not understand the diagnosis, but I did understand that his condition was potentially life-threatening, and there was little anyone could do. My seemingly healthy son was going to undergo more medical testing, and it was going to be involved.

Even though I had a college degree by then, I was lucky to have an entry level job at the state employment agency. I looked around at some of my highly educated co-workers and realized jobs were hard to find in Scottsdale, Arizona. I knew I should be grateful and be careful to please the boss. I was trying to function, but my emotions were out of control. I'll never forget how broken and hopeless I felt.

Our little family was in a state of upheaval even before the diagnosis. My husband and I were discontented, and had just moved to Arizona. It was a move similar to the one we made from New York City to the Midwest seven years earlier. We did not have jobs, or a home, or even big plans. We just took our things, and went to search for better opportunities. I suppose we were acting out our version of the pioneer spirit of our country. The biggest difference with this move was that we had a child.

I know that many people move with children, but I thought our son was special. My mother always reminded me, "Every crow thinks hers is the blackest." I guess that is human nature, but I had had some difficulties that most do not have in producing one son. I had lost one pregnancy at age twenty-two that sent me into a very long depression. It was a wound I carried, and a dark thread in the weaving of my life.

I worried the entire time I was pregnant the second time. It had not been easy, and I was five weeks and two days past my given due date when I finally had my baby on October 17, 1973. I was told all was well with him, but things were far from well with me. Another wound. I remember how happy I was to see my baby as I came to consciousness on the delivery room table. I did not realize yet what had happened to me—complications. It would be twelve days before I was well enough to leave the hospital, and many weeks and months of recovery were ahead of me. More difficulties and depression followed.

We named our long-awaited son John Wesley, and I often told him that he was "the apple of my eye." He had a delightful personality and the natural buoyancy of a child. His Dad and I were his devoted fans. He was rarely sick, and never had a bad report until the diagnosis in Scottsdale. He was not even sick then. We had only taken him to the doctor because it was near the time for his yearly check up, and he had a cough. I thought it was nothing serious and it wasn't—at least not the cough. However, what the tests eventually confirmed was neurofibromatosis. It was genetic—my son had been born with it.

You do not believe, you bargain, you sink into hopelessness. At least that was the only way I seemed capable of responding to the devastating news. I look back and recognize that I was going through a grieving process. At the time, it felt like the rawest wound I could imagine because it affected the most loved little human being in my life. I remember looking at him as a newborn, and knowing he was a gift from God. There was no other way to explain it. He was without a doubt the happiest thing that ever had happened to me. Thoughts swirled in my head. *How could God let this happen? What will this mean for my son's life? Is this punishment for me? What am I going to do?* I was supposed to protect my son and make certain he had a good life. This disease was out of my control.

Wes was a happy, well-adjusted child. He was not sick, and he could not understand why I cried so much. His dad concealed his grief, and tried to pretend all the tests were "no big deal." I tried. My grief was evident in the tears that streamed down my face most of the time. I attempted to veil my sadness, but it was usually written all over my face.

Depressive moods were not new to me. They were the dark threads of my life. It did not take much to trigger a downward spiral. A headache would do. Still, this heartbreaking situation was the worst blow in my life.

At the time, I was the breadwinner in the family. We did not have health insurance. I was new at my job and did not dare ask for time off. Even though I felt like rolling in a ball and pulling the covers over my head, I had to go to the office. My tears were out of control.

The day after the devastating diagnosis, I arrived at work professionally dressed with make-up on, presentable to the public. My tears had dried. I might have looked good on the outside, but my heart was broken inside. If I kept my mind on my work, I was only aware of a hovering sadness. When my mind strayed to the frightening possibilities for my son, I lost control and cried. I didn't feel like I could even excuse myself and go to the ladies' room, because there was no one to cover my desk. Tears and tissues became a way of life.

Every way I turned, I felt trapped. Trapped by the prognosis— "Nothing can be done. We'll just deal with the symptoms." Financially trapped by my job. No place to turn. No hope. I prayed to God. I never heard anything from God though. There was no hope in that for me. Still, it was the only hope I had, so I continued to pray. Would God hear this time and would things get better?

The tears that began the day of the diagnosis continued for many years. They were mixed with an inner loneliness I had been unable to escape. They also were the jumpstart to begin my journey to becoming serious about God. I began to consider going to church again.

Corrie said that in her later years, she was more in control of her tears. I have found that to be true for me as well. However, I am now thankful for my tears. They have been healing and were a critical factor in my search for God and his plan. How long would I search and cry before I found him?

John Wesley Czarnota at age ten months

The Weaving

A Night of Surrender

I walked out the door of my pastor's office to drive home. I thought about my new assignments, new things I was learning, and my painful personal problems. My mind was busy trying to grasp it all. The pastor had volunteered to counsel me. I did not feel too good about that. I felt a little guilty and undeserving of his time. Honestly, I feared counseling would not do any good. The pastor was already so busy with teaching school, pastoring a small church, and being a husband and father to his wife and four kids.

When I met the pastor, I was stopped by the fact that he had four kids. It had not been that many years since I read *The Population Bomb*. Wasn't it common knowledge that no one was supposed to have more than one or two kids? I thought it seemed like a fair and reasonable warning that we were overpopulating the world. My parents had certainly done their share by having seven children. When I lived in New York and talked and worried about the danger of overpopulation, my Polish mother-in-law had spoken in her broken English that we could just stack the people in high-rises. She was not worried. Her attitude made me worry all the more, along with others in my generation who were "enlightened" about this danger.

The fact was that no one I knew in my age bracket had four kids. This pastor was only four years younger than me. Where did he get permission to have four kids? I was intrigued by the kid issue. At first, it spoke louder to me than anything he said. I could tell he was different. He sure was not playing by the rules of the culture we lived in. I admired that. I paid attention to what he said to figure out what was behind his views that made his choices different.

I had not been a regular churchgoer since I was a young teenager at home. I became too busy. Maybe it just was not cool enough. After I went to college, I did not know anyone who bothered to go to church. Church was the old days—hypocrites and all.

But life has a way of getting your attention—mine, at least. I had experienced some major heartache by the time I returned to church. Serious things—not only did my son have potentially life-threatening medical problems that weren't going away, but my subsequent divorce from his Dad had rocked his world in a damaging way. My second marriage was in trouble, giving me and my son more emotional pain than I had bargained for.

My second husband and I sought professional counseling, and we were told that there was not much hope of us reconciling our differences. That was not the answer I wanted to hear, but I feared it was right. I was angry and depressed. My stubborn will was set on making the marriage work. I did not want to fail again. My moods swung from resignation to brief periods of hope. The evening I spoke with the pastor I was holding some shred of hope that God could help my situation.

I had previously tried to talk my pastor out of counseling me, "Oh, that's okay, there's not much hope for us." I went to him to talk about my failing marriage because it seemed to be the biggest issue at the time.

The pastor insisted confidently, "No, I think I can help you."

I had agreed to go for counseling and did not want to waste his time. I could not take his advice half-heartedly. I had to be committed.

I was pretty much out of ideas for my happiness. Earlier I decided that I should try to read the Bible. I believed in God, and I believed the Bible was God's word. I grabbed an old Bible my aunt gave me in 1963, and tried to read it. But there were so many problems consuming my mind, I could not follow what I was reading long enough to make sense of it.

I had been praying to God ever since my son's diagnosis in 1977. It had not helped much that I could tell, but I kept praying—just in case it might help. There did not seem to be much choice.

I made a decision to go back to church—not just go, but commit to go, really meaning it. It was time for me to get serious.

Occasionally, I picked up some free leaflets at the back of church. They were compelling topics, and always ended in committing to Jesus. I read through them, and hoped I had said and done all they explained about the way to God. I thought about those leaflets as I drove home from my counseling session that night. There was a place to sign and date them. I had not done that before because I did not know any specific date I could put down. It was not really clear to me.

I decided to ask my pastor to explain salvation the evening he counseled me. I realized I was a little fuzzy on the particulars. I heard people ask, "Is she saved? Are they saved?" Those questions bugged me, so I asked my pastor to explain. I do not remember exactly what he said, but I responded with another question that popped up in my mind, "Do you think I'm not saved?" I remember clearly that he told me I could make sure of it by making a decision, and going forward from that day.

I started praying from the time I left my counseling session. I prayed on the way home. Whatever it would take to get right with God, I was ready to do it. I was weary. I was troubled. I had problems that I knew no one on earth could solve. I felt that God was my only solution. I had all I could stand of hurt, disappointment, and heartache.

I asked God to direct me if he wanted me to pull the car over, and pray about my decision even before I got home. I did not hear any answer or have a feeling, so I kept driving. When I got home, I told my husband what the pastor told me. He said he guessed it did not work like a seniority roster with God, and I had nothing to lose. His comments encouraged me. He did not realize the seriousness of my decision, or the effect my newfound zeal would have on our relationship.

I found and signed those leaflets from church when I got home. I reviewed the elements. I knew that I was a sinner and, of course, I was sorry for my sins. I believed in Jesus and wanted him to be my Savior. I signed two of the leaflets just to make sure. I thought, *Oh, what could ink on paper mean?* Still, I wrote my name and the date—September 16, 1983.

In my bed in the dark that night, I kept praying. I had the uneasy feeling that even though I knew and believed the statements of faith in the leaflets, there was something I missed. My heart cried, "I give up. I have made a mess of my life, but I give it to you. If you can do anything with it, it's yours. I'm not going my way any longer." I meant that with my whole heart. I sensed it was the most radical thing I had ever done in my life. Hadn't I always admired people with the guts to be radical? My way—my culture's way—had not worked for me. I just had to do something, and I felt signing those leaflets was the right thing. I felt a release. It felt revolutionary, and that was exciting. I was free somehow. I did not understand it. But sometime later a feeling of peace settled over me, and I went to sleep.

In the days and weeks after that night, I knew my prayer was heard. Joy began to grow inside me. First, I noticed people at the hospital where I worked smiling at me. I thought it was strange, because they had not smiled at me before. When I thought that through, I realized it was because I had first smiled at them. The smiles let me know for sure that God had heard, and Jesus was really in my heart. Somehow, he was giving me a peace and joy that my life had lacked. The joy that I began to feel was my encouragement that there was a God, and he had heard me. It was the fruit of my pivotal prayer of surrender.

Did my prayer change my marriage? It changed everything in my life, but not in ways I understood. Tension in my marriage did not decrease—it increased. My son's medical problems were not going away. Frequent hospital stays, medicine, tests, and trips to doctors continued. With my depressive habits and serious nature, the joy I felt was a miracle to me. It was as shiny as a diamond on a black display cloth. It had not come from me. It was from God!

Knowing that God heard my prayer and was healing the hurt in my heart allowed me a freedom I had never known before. I was different inside. The core of me that was confused and hurting started healing. I did not understand it. I had a lot to learn, and the days ahead weren't going to be easy. I began to read and understand the Bible. I was committed to going to church and opening my heart to a new way to live. One special person would come into my life very soon to help point the way for me and I met her in a movie.

The Movie

It was a Sunday evening in 1984 when I got behind the wheel of my Volkswagen to drive alone to my small church in suburban Kansas City. It did not matter to me what the activity was because I had resolved to go and be a part of everything. It had been less than a year since my night of surrender.

I was excited as I pulled into the parking lot because God was giving me new eyes and ears to understand spiritual truths. The building was an aging rented structure that had been a church before our newly formed group occupied it. It was cool and pleasant inside, even though it was a bit shabby. The people were friendly, and I counted them as my new Christian friends. The meeting began, as always, with singing, and our young preacher accompanied us on his guitar. However, this particular evening there was not a normal service. Instead, a movie would be shown.

The lights were dimmed, and *The Hiding Place* began. I noticed that the film was made by the Billy Graham organization, which impressed me because I had admired him for years. The movie reenacted the true story of Corrie ten Boom's Holocaust experience. It was the history of a time that I had not studied much. War-torn Holland and Germany seemed far away from the middle-class America where I lived. I had never heard of Corrie, but I was paying close attention. There were so many Christians and Christian beliefs that were new to me. I wondered if I would ever catch up with the other members of the congregation.

I watched with many thoughts going through my mind. *I thought it was the Jews who were put in camps in the Holocaust. Were there others?* The story that unfolded on the screen was about a Christian family that chose to reach out to the Jews in a way that clearly endangered their lives.

Father ten Boom even wanted to show his support of the Jews by wearing the armband that Jews were forced to wear! The middle-aged spinster sisters chose to work in the Dutch underground to provide food and a hiding place for Jews until they could be transported to safe havens in the Dutch countryside. In order to help, Corrie and Betsie had to practice deception that was very foreign to their Christian upbringing. Corrie, Betsie, and Father ten Boom were people that I quickly began to admire for their unwavering courage and commitment to God and the Jews.

As the film showed the Ten Booms being arrested and eventually taken to the concentration camp, my heart hurt for them. The scenes in the camp were so horrific, it turned my stomach. The guards were brutal, and the prisoners were filthy and starving. I wondered if I could have survived those conditions.

Father and Betsie died, but Corrie was miraculously released. My heart rejoiced as she walked out of that prison. I wondered what would be left of her life. She was old and sick and now alone. I wondered how this could have a happy ending.

The old woman who came on the screen at the end to talk about the movie was not an actress, but the real Corrie ten Boom. I studied her lined, aged face with the warm, lively eyes. I was looking at Corrie's face more than listening to what she said. She radiated joy and peace. I found her facial expression even more compelling than her words. Her sincerity hit my heart as real, and confirmed the love I read in her eyes. Her face was beautiful to me because of that love. I wanted to be near her and sit at her feet. I wanted her to tell me more of her story, and ask how God brought her through it. The Ten Booms had risked their lives to live their faith. They put their money where their mouth was and suffered the consequences. That kind of guts charged me up.

As the lights came on, my surroundings came into focus, the movie was over, and it was time to go home. I picked up my purse, retrieving my keys, and soberly walked alone back to my car. Traveling the miles back to my empty and lonely home, I played the scenes over and over in my mind. I knew I was in training with God, and I wanted to learn from this movie. A real life story of someone who had lived her Christian principles could be an example for me. I liked the fact that she was just an ordinary person that God used. That detail gave me hope. I loved seeing her as an old woman, still believing and holding on to her faith. In my mind, it was one thing to be charged up with convictions when you are young, but quite another to maintain those convictions and enthusiasm until the twilight of your life.

To me, there is nothing like the peace and joy in an old wrinkled face. I wanted to learn from someone older. I believed Corrie knew something about living the Christian life that I needed to know. She had suffered, but had not lost her faith. I wished I could find out more. God was going to make that wish come true. He had already prepared me—in my childhood.

Meet Little Evelyn

As I pulled the small, vintage wooden frame out of the package, I knew I was in for a treat because it was a gift from an artistic friend. The glass in the frame had not survived the trip from Arkansas to Kansas City. But, beneath the broken pieces of glass was a counted cross-stitch embroidery of a small child in an upholstered chair with a book on her lap.

My friend Laura was an artist and had entered a new embroidery phase in her artistic expressions. I loved her eye for simple, forgotten vintage treasures and her knack for putting them into use again. The Depression-era frame was fragile. It had a small wire eye to slip over a nail. I imagined it on an old, papered wall in a small home many years ago. The new style embroidery brought it into the present. The upholstered chair in the cross-stitch appeared to be from the Depression era—much like some of my own furniture.

When I spoke to Laura she explained, "That's you, little Evelyn." She had chosen light yellow thread for the hair of the child which resembled my haircolor. Laura reminded me that I had told her how much I read as a child, and how my life had been shaped by books. She always made me feel that I was unique and interesting.

During my childhood, Mama's often heard remark was "Evelyn's always got her head in a book." This was not a comment of her pride in me. On the contrary, it was her lament. There was way too much work to be done in my family for anyone to be too idle.

I did not blame Mama. I was being idle by reading. Sometimes, I was trying to get out of doing dishes, cleaning, or babysitting my younger siblings. I was even trying to get away from people. I was trying to get away from my siblings or the sometime uncomfortable presence of my dominating father. I was trying to find myself a place in books that made more sense. Books provided a more orderly world, a happier family, a place far away from the ordinariness of my world growing up in Kansas City in the 1950s.

How did I come to taking company with books, preferring them at times to people? Years later my father provided me with a glimpse of "Little Evelyn" from his memories of my earliest years. Daddy was on a descent into dementia when he told me this story but he had a moment in time that seemed very clear to him. He remembered that my older, more gregarious sister was running and playing with the neighborhood children. Daddy found me in the sandbox in the back yard. I had a jar and scoop and was busy and happy. He watched while I put sand in the bottle, and then poured it out so I could fill it again—over and over. Daddy said he wondered why I would pursue that monotony, asking me, "Little Evelyn, don't you want to go and play with the other kids?" He remembered that I just continued my fascination with the sand.

Daddy was a man who pondered things, but maybe I did not realize that because he was so vocal and outgoing. Mama tended towards shyness—in public at least—and was way too busy to ponder, managing her brood of children and meeting the demands of my father.

I was, in Daddy's words, his "number two daughter," and my brother came along a short eighteen months after me. In that lineup, there was not much time for individual connection with my father. There was always a younger child who drew his attention—which was pretty much fine with me.

Daddy could be very hard to please and demanding of perfection that none of us could reach. He could quickly become angry. I sensed that it was in my best interests to blend in, and not come under his direct scrutiny which would sometimes bring his wrath. Mama taught us by word and example, "Daddy loves you kids." I accepted that as the truth. It rang true in my gut. But knowing Daddy loved me did not make living with his changing moods easy. It was easier for me to escape in a book and stay out of the way.

I believe Daddy's memory in a moment of clarity was a gift from God to me. I never considered that Daddy pondered scenes about me in his mind. It was a revelation to me about him, and helpful to see him as a thoughtful man. It was also a confirmation to me that my sometimes introverted personality today had manifested itself in my unconscious childhood activities.

My older sister taught me to read. I wanted to be as big and as smart as she was. That sibling rivalry was in place from the beginning. Whatever Margaret learned, she was out to teach and help the less enlightened ones around her—that would be me. God's grace was in that because I learned to read before other children my age.

That skill put me at the top of my class by the time I started school. In addition to reading, I also learned to be more outgoing from my sister. I watched as she told stories and interacted with kids and I tried to imitate her.

However at home, I escaped into books. I was the only one at home who read much—except for my father. Back then I think his reading was confined to the evening paper, because he was busy as he shouldered the weight of earning a living for a growing family. As an adult, I realize that entailed some conformity that would not come naturally to this intelligent and opinionated man. Perhaps my own tendency to be a non-conformist can be traced to Daddy.

As I reflected on the embroidery that my friend Laura made, I recognized there were some differences from the reality of my busy childhood home. The cross-stitched little girl was sitting properly in a nice chair in a living area. That would never have been me at home. I usually preferred to be in the bedroom on the bed or the floor. Sometimes Mama would shoo us outside to play. I was never athletic, so often I would end up reading on the steps of the porch or on a quilt under a tree to read.

My friend's thoughtful gift communicated to me that she honored who I was, and that I had become the person she liked because of my reading. I embraced that nod of approval. I felt like I perceived the world differently than many people. My fascination with books played a critical role in developing my character. The world as I experienced it had been shaped by books.

Years later, I remembered my friend's embroidery piece and searched through boxes in my garage until I found it. I wanted to honor the message and artistry of my friend. I finally had the glass replaced, and wrote on the paper that sealed up the back, "Little

Evelyn" by Laura Niccoli Hudson, 1980s. I regretted not recording the specific date I received it. Today, that embroidery piece and its vintage frame have an honored place on my office bookcase.

I study the muted colors that my friend chose to embroider the scene—how perfectly they fit the frame. Her artistic eye is a gift I admire. Corrie was a gifted storyteller and used that gift in her speaking and writing. Both women inspire me to find my gifts, and use them to encourage others.

Reflecting on my past, I see that life is precious and filled with God's grace and traces of his weaving—even though I could not see it at the time. Now, I see that God was shaping me in my childhood interests. It would be through reading that I would be prepared to meet Corrie. It is only backwards that I can catch a glimpse of his hand preparing my path. I had no idea that my enjoyment of reading would become the way I would connect with Corrie.

Evelyn at age seven.

The family at Easter, 1955.
Aaron and Marie Cleaver with Margaret,
Evelyn, Alan, and Joyce.

The Weaving

Trusting God to Guide

One morning my mission was to get some exercise at the local mall. I was making my laps around, but also scanning the store windows as I passed. The window at the Christian book store especially beckoned me to come in. I devoured books from the time I first learned to read. I found it was one of the best ways for me to learn. Now that I am on to Christianity I reasoned, surely a book would help me learn. I would just see what God might lead me to find.

I finished my laps, walked back to the store, and my eyes began to scan the shelves. I was learning to trust God to lead me. My heart was praying that I would see what I needed to see as my eyes caught sight of that face. It was the woman I met in the movie at church— Corrie ten Boom! I knew she could teach me something about living the Christian life. She had that same peace and joy on her face I saw in the movie. I could not wait to read her story in the pages of that book.

I paid for that paperback copy of *Tramp for the Lord* and left the mall with great expectations for the treasure I had found. I looked forward to filling my lonely evenings with the companionship of a new book and a new friend. In another century, Emily Dickinson wrote, "There is no frigate like a book to take you to lands far away." Books had been my ticket away from my circumstances since the 1950s. I couldn't wait to take the ride.

I was on a new revolutionary adventure with Christ. I sensed his guidance directing me to Corrie's book. It continued her story of the years that began where the movie left off. In the book I became acquainted with the traveling Corrie. I love to travel, so that connected me right away to my new friend. When I read, I always try to construct the scenes in my mind like a movie. I watch the movie as I read. In visualizing this old woman with her suitcase, I tried to imagine the faith and resolve it took to begin her travels at age fifty-three and continue them for the next thirty-three years.

Corrie wrote about her first visit to New York right after the war. She did not know anyone. She only had some addresses to contact. One memorable scene for me took place at the YWCA where Corrie was told she could not stay any longer. She had very little money and no place else to stay, but she had confidence that God had directed her there. A letter arrived later that very day with an offer of hospitality from a woman who had attended one of Corrie's lectures. It was a happy provision of God. Her child-like trust that God was leading her was rewarded.

I had lived in New York City years before, and knew it could be an intimidating place. It can be frightening to be alone anywhere—let alone in a foreign country. I thought, *How did she hold on to her confidence and faith? Look at the timing of God to send her another home to stay in just exactly on the day she needed it!* The stories I read in the book challenged me to trust God more and more. I wanted to be as fearless as Corrie, but I knew I had a long way to go.

Corrie described some of the opposition she faced at the beginning of her ministry. Many counseled her to go home and forget about her experiences during the war. They scoffed at the idea that Corrie had been led by the Lord to tell about what she had learned. She wrote about a Christian man who encouraged her by saying, "Pay no attention to them (the naysayers). The Bible contains many promises that God will lead those who obey him. Have you ever heard of a good shepherd who does not lead his sheep?"

I read about Corrie's faith and belief in the direct guidance of God. It all sounded so easy. We trust, God provides. I wondered if she second-guessed herself like I do sometimes. I knew my own impatience and fear. I wondered how she felt while she was waiting. I had questions. I wanted to apply what I was learning to my life. I knew there were spiritual principles there, and I was trying hard to understand.

I liked to travel, but I also knew how difficult it could be. Often I found it tiring, never sleeping as well as I did in my own bed. Sometimes eating strange food can be hard to digest. Sitting long hours on airplanes, trains, or buses was challenging for my much younger body. How did Corrie do it well into her eighties? I was hooked on her story and wanted to know more.

I wanted so much to have Corrie's child-like trust. I believed God was in the miracle-working business. I vowed to trust him to change me more, so I could do his will. I resolved to believe that God was near and working in my life. I underlined Corrie's and her parents' life verse in my Bible:

*I will instruct you and teach you in the way which you should
go; I will counsel you with my eye upon you.*

Psalms 32:8 NASB

It became my heart's prayer. I wanted to see his hand and be
directed by him.

When I reflected on my past, I marveled at how God heard that
prayer and guided me into ministry. In rereading the passage about
the naysayers, I could feel Corrie's pain in a way that I did not
know when I first read the book. I heard discouraging words as
well. Just because I believed God directed me did not mean others
would see it that way. I had to learn to hold on to what I learned
from Corrie.

When visiting with a friend over a cup of coffee at our local
Starbucks, I was marveling at how people's problems seem to run
in the same vein. Anita reminded me, "Satan is really not that
creative. He uses the same old things." Yes, of course, he is the
opposite of the Great Creator. Why do I fall for his lies? A Good
Shepherd does lead the sheep.

Corrie was born into a Dutch family in Holland and lived in
another generation, but I experienced the same lies from the pit of
hell that she wrote about. I felt a kinship with her that transcended
our differences. God guided Corrie, and he guided me. My eyes
searched for my next step.

A Spiritual Grandmother

There she was! Corrie's eyes smiled at me from her photo on the cover of a small paperback copy of *Each New Day*. She was sitting at a table with some needlework in her hands. The Bible was open in front of her. I imagined myself sitting across from her at that table. I was excited to think that she could speak to me through that book. I believed even God could speak to me through it.

In May of 1985, I found myself again searching the shelves at a Christian book store. Corrie had become a closer friend through *Tramp for the Lord*, so I was on the lookout for any more books she had written. Books were often my friends. I reached for books to fill the lonely places in my life. In those days, there were many lonely times. I had the recurring pain from a divorce, a hurtful, estranged second marriage, a difficult job, and worry over my son's incurable medical problems. Once again, I sought companionship and counsel in a book.

I purchased my second Corrie ten Boom book and took it home to enjoy. My heart was hungry for the message of the May 20 devotional in *Each New Day*:

> There were three times in my life when prison locks were closed behind me. It was very difficult. Many of us experience locks closed behind us at times when we have almost insurmountable problems. I learned, and you will learn, that that means a difficult class in life's school. But you can learn much, especially when the teacher is able. My teacher was the Lord, and He is willing to be yours.

> *Show me Your ways, O Lord; teach me Your paths. Lead me in Your truth, and teach me: for You are the God of my salvation; on You do I wait all the day.* Psalms 25:4-5 KJV

> We are Your willing pupils, Lord. The classroom is of Your choosing, the lessons only part of Your plan for us. Thank You that Your Holy Spirit teaches us how to be willing to study in Your school.

I underlined the line that was the prayer of my heart. I prayed, "I want to be a willing student in your classroom, Lord." I received a lifetime teaching certificate from my college education but I knew how frustrating and futile it could be to try to teach someone who would not cooperate.

In my current situation, I was not in a position of authority. I was not the teacher, but the student. I wanted to cooperate with God. I believed he was teaching me through Corrie's experiences.

Reading *Each New Day* was like a one-way conversation with Corrie. That was fine with me because I was sick of my own ideas.

This was my time to *listen*. My eyes were riveted on each page. Every fiber of my being listened to Corrie in that book.

I put my copy of *Each New Day* on the oak cabinet of the antique treadle sewing machine that served as a bedside table. My bed was my favorite reading spot, and I always kept a Bible there, along with a book or two. I added Corrie's book to my daily reading. It stayed at my bedside for years. Corrie became my mentor, a spiritual grandmother, a friend, and a companion, as she taught me through her writings. I picked up the book for counsel like I might have picked up the phone to call a friend who cared about me. She helped me put my problems in perspective. I reminded myself that even though I had a lot of problems, at least I was not in a concentration camp. The message came through—Corrie made it; you can make it.

The advantage of this book was that it was in measured meals. Most books I gobbled up, zooming through them to see what happened and what I could learn. I always have that appetite to learn and I tend to gobble as I read. This book was different because it had a short devotion for each day of the year. I could just take just one serving a day and savor it.

I was hungry to learn how other people lived the Christian life and overcame their difficulties. The Bible tells us that if we walk with the wise, we will become wise. I found that I was becoming wise because I was walking with Corrie in her books.

Remember your leaders, who spoke the word of God to you. Consider the outcome of their way of life and imitate their faith. Hebrews 13:7 NIV

Corrie wrote the following thoughts in *The Hiding Place*:

...books do not age as you and I do. They will speak still
when we are gone, to generations we will never see. Yes, the
books must survive.

Corrie was quoting an old rabbi from her hometown of Haarlem
in conversation with her father. Those words ring as true today as
when they were spoken in Holland during World War II. Her
books remained to allow me and the generations coming behind
her to consider her way of life. I marveled at how God prepared
her and used her suffering to help me. Corrie spoke to me each day
in her books, and taught me to believe that God would be with me
and guide me. I had some years of difficult days ahead, but
brighter ones were not too far away.

Pay Attention

"I don't know what you're thinking. I'm too old to be your girlfriend, but if you want to be just friends…" I blurted out to my new acquaintance from work. I had just arrived at his doorstep as we had planned. Where did I earn the right to be that blunt? Rob was twelve years younger than me, for Pete's sake. I did not know him that well. I had only talked with him a few minutes in the morning when our shifts at work overlapped. He was friendly and seemed kind and maybe just lonely.

I was weary from dating disasters and always looking for clues to let me know men's real motives. I really hated dating. My second divorce had been final for about four years. I knew I needed to socialize more, but dating was so different now. I was a Christian, and I knew that I wanted to marry a Christian. There sure did not seem to be many Christian men around me to choose from. I did not want to waste any time on men who did not share my faith.

Oh sure, they all claimed to be Christians. I had to constantly search for clues to tell me what their words did not.

I was grieving. My second marriage had ended in divorce despite all my prayers for the marriage to be healed. God had not changed my husband's decision. I had *believed* God could and would intervene. I had to accept that God was right, and I just did not understand. That was not easy for me. In my prayers, I asked God to choose a husband for me. I had chosen two and those marriages had failed. I did not want to repeat any more failures.

My dreams of teaching had long since been sidelined. Instead, I worked the day shift at Trans World Airlines' aircraft maintenance facility. My son needed medical treatment that was available out of the country. I had taken a job with the airline for the flight privileges to get my son the treatment he needed. I needed to make a living too, and the job paid more than teaching school. I had become a licensed avionics mechanic. However, the stress of working in a field where I had very little talent was exhausting. I was weary.

I was also grieving the death of a close friend. Vicki had been my friend since we were both fourteen. She was divorced and working just like me. We had a lot of things in common. A year earlier, from out of nowhere, she was diagnosed with pancreatic cancer. I visited her and shared as much as I could of the last year of her life. We studied the Bible together. I sat by her bed as she took her last breath. It was a loss that sent me further into depression.

I was grieving and depressed, not rude, the day I first visited Rob's house. I needed to get out of the house. I recognized the familiar signs of depression. If I stayed at home, I would be in my nightgown by four in the afternoon. I had little contact with people outside the guys I worked with and my church on Sundays.

Rob offered to take me out to eat and I thought, "Well, that wouldn't kill me." I decided to take that little step. I wondered how he would deal with me and my frankness when I decided to just cut to the chase. Most guys I knew would have made a scene of some kind but instead, Rob just looked at me in silence with an expression that was hard to read. I did not want to be cruel and hurt him. I also did not want him to get the wrong idea and have expectations of me.

Rob's simple, Depression-era home was in a thinly populated area not far from my new duplex in suburbia. I could tell from that first visit that this guy was a little different. He did not have clutter around. His home was furnished sparsely, monk-like. When I asked where his TV was, he said he did not have one.

"Where are *you* from?" was my next question. I didn't know any normal men who did not have a TV. He immediately caught the humor of the way I worded my question and played along, "Granite City, Illinois." I liked that. I made him laugh.

That first visit led to one after another. One day I was visiting and decided to just nose around his house a little. I noticed a Bible with a worn-out cover tucked by the padded railing of his water bed. "Pay attention," were the words I heard inside me as I caught a glimpse of myself in the mirror of a built in chest of drawers.

My thoughts were racing. *Is this the man I've been praying for? Is he really reading the Bible? Is he a true believer? But he's so young! How can this work?* Thoughts tumbled around and around in my head, but I knew I had heard the quiet admonition to settle down and watch.

Listening was something I was learning at work too. I was working in a field where I often did not even know an intelligent question to ask. I had to listen and pay attention, and hope I would catch on. That was uncomfortable for me because I would rather just talk. I liked to be in control and sure of myself. Life was teaching me that I was not in control. I had to make the effort to be intelligent enough to pay attention.

Despite my early reservations, Rob and I were more compatible than I could imagine. We began a year of dating. It had to be God. Rob would need endless patience to deal with a depressed and wounded, but still headstrong woman. I needed to heal and trust. But God was up for challenges like that. Sometimes I sensed God's pleasure in the challenge. All I knew was that he was weaving some of the happier threads in my life. The years ahead would reveal how crucial this man would be to God's plans for me.

Evelyn at T.W.A. instrument shop

Ability or Availability

"God is not looking for your ability, but your availability!" the earthy and fiery evangelist thundered. I was sitting near the back that evening in a revival service in my church's auditorium. I had been considering what God would have me do with all the newfound time on my hands since I had moved to Oklahoma with my new husband. Everything was new in my life. I did not have a full-time job for the first time in years. I seemed to have endless possibilities.

My friend Vicki's death in 1989 gave me a fresh realization of how short life really was. I also knew that I was not doing what I had been put on earth to do. Airline work was only a temporary sideline. I felt an urgency to find my calling, and get busy doing what God had created me for. I knew I needed to be accountable for my time and all God had been teaching me.

Ever since I bought my first Bob Dylan album in 1966, I found that he always seemed to have a song that spoke of the things that I was thinking. After I became a Christian the lyrics of *What Can I Do For You?* played in my head as I longed to serve God and make my time count.

> *What can I do for You?*
> *You have given everything to me*
> *What can I do for You?*
> *You have given me eyes to see*
> *What can I do for You?*
> *I know all about poison,*
> *I know all about fiery darts*
> *I don't care how rough the road is,*
> *Show me where it starts*
> *Whatever pleases You,*
> *Tell it to my heart*
> *Well, I don't deserve it,*
> *But I sure did make it through*
> *What can I do for You?*

Rob and I married in 1991 after one wonderful year of courtship. Shortly afterwards, I asked him if I could quit my job. He did not take time to think about it, but simply answered, "Yes, if you want to." I quit my job, and began to get busy at homemaking work that I had long dreamed of having the time to do.

The next year Rob and I moved to Oklahoma when he took a job with American Airlines. My son had graduated high school by then and seemed content in Missouri. We left all our family and friends behind as we set out to forge our new future together. I secretly hoped that God might allow us to have a child to raise together.

That hope died slowly as my biological clock ticked, and I suffered two miscarriages.

I trusted that God had a plan, and I was trying hard to find out what it was. I tried to reason what I might do for him. I also knew God's ways were not my ways, so I had to be open to new ideas. I spent most of my time keeping my home, gardening, learning to cook, entertaining, and volunteering at church. I didn't feel like it needed to be any grandiose feat for God. Just working at making my home inviting and reaching out to people would be enough. After all, I learned years ago that *life was about people, not stuff.*

The evangelist's phrase stuck in my heart. God was not looking for my abilities, he was looking for my availability. I felt like I was on shaky ground when it came to looking at my abilities, but my availability was a choice. I thought, *What can I do that will be useful to God?* That was unclear to me, but I was clearly available. I wrote the evangelist's phrase in the back of my Bible. It was comforting to me. My working and trying hard and pondering could relax a little. I decided to pray and remind God, "I'm available." That prayer did not seem like much at the time, but I meant it with my whole heart. I began to keep my eyes open for every opportunity to serve God.

The Weaving

An Idea
Out of the Blue

"How did you ever get started portraying Corrie ten Boom?" It was a reasonable question and one I heard frequently. The idea for my performance and the most specific answer involves a story about when I was busy with another project. I suppose it is not so different than many other times in our lives where one thing leads to another and before you know it, you are on a different path.

In 1996 I was a volunteer docent and tour guide at the Philbrook Art Museum in Tulsa, Oklahoma. I had been interested in art museums for as long as I could remember, and I was fulfilling a dream of having the time to help others enjoy art as I did. I became fascinated with the story of one of the prominent donors of the museum's collection. I offered to interview this woman's family and prepare a lecture that I could present to the new docents-in-training.

When I contacted the museum's director of education to set up a date for my presentation, she suggested, seemingly out of the blue, "Why don't you dress up like her?" She told me she thought that might be a fun addition to my talk. Part of the draw of being a volunteer was the entertaining projects and skits we had. It had not occurred to me before, but it seemed reasonable the moment she said it. I often have to be able to visualize myself doing something before I agree to do it. That day I did not hesitate. In my mind's eye, I saw myself in costume and boldly reassured her, "Oh sure, I can do that."

To understand why dressing up in costume appealed to me, I looked back at the threads woven during my days in my high school. I debuted as an actress on a college stage when I was seventeen. At that time, I divided my time between college classes and finishing my senior year in high school. A professor who became my mentor directed plays at the college. Jenkin David was not only a good teacher and director, but he was known for his eye for casting. I reminded him of one of his own daughters who started college before she finished high school just as I had done. Mr. David thought I had potential and gave me one of the lead roles in a college play, even though I had never been on the stage. I had a lot of respect for him, and he had confidence in me. He inspired me. Without realizing it, I became determined to rise to the occasion and fulfill his vision. I could not let him down since he believed in me.

I had really never thought about acting before I met Jenkin David. I saw myself as more academic and focused on literature. The amazing thing I discovered was the electricity that I felt on stage. Mr. David gave me a lead role and had a formal shiny red satin dress especially tailored for me for one dramatic scene. I had been well cast in my part and was determined to do well. I will never forget when I stepped on the stage in that stunning dress. I felt the electricity of passion and creativity, and that feeling hooked me. At the time, I did not think in terms of being gifted by God. I just realized from what I felt and people's reactions that I was good at it, and I loved performing.

I remembered that feeling when my teaching opportunity at the museum gave me an opportunity to act. I had already studied to get a sense of museum donor Laura Clubb's values and personality from articles and an interview with her granddaughter. I changed my report to a monologue to inspire the docents and give them a sense of the colorful woman with a strong personality.

I was familiar with the photos I had seen of Mrs. Clubb and I knew that my costume would be critical. She was a large woman with big round tortoise-shell glasses and wore lots of beaded necklaces. I still had a pair of glasses from my high school days that would work perfectly. I had necklaces so that would be easy. My dress was my biggest concern.

A friend from church had given me a tip that she had seen a rack of vintage clothes at a Goodwill store in Tulsa. I became a woman on a mission. I found the rack of clothes near the back of the shop. It was so crowded that there was little room to scoot the hangers to look at each dress. I went through each one quickly and assigned them, in my mind, to their decade. I needed something that screamed '50s.

"This is it," I thought while surveying a nicely sewn homemade party dress. It was navy taffeta with a straight skirt that came to my mid-calf. It was an appropriately large enough size, but it was slightly low cut in front and even more so in the back. I knew that would not work, but thought I could solve the problem with a lace shell under it. I could cover the back with a fur stole that I planned to borrow from another docent. The crowning touch to this dress was that it had a hand-beaded vintage pin sewn on it that clearly set it in the 1950s. The six-dollar price tag sealed the deal for me. It was perfect for Mrs. Clubb, and it was soon to become useful as my costume for Corrie.

As I came off the stage that morning as Laura Clubb in the impressive theater at the Philbrook, I was energized with the same feeling I had from performing years ago. Many people came up to me with excited praise for my performance. One comment from Laura Clubb's family, touched my heart, "I think Grandmother would be proud. You've captured her spirit." I felt immediately like this was a God thing.

My friend Patty Raulston accompanied me to the museum that morning to watch my performance. She helped me gather my things afterwards. I did not even take time to change my costume before heading home. We had a twenty-five mile drive from the museum to my home in Claremore, so we had time to laugh and wonder at the excitement my performance had generated. We went to the same church and were involved in the planning of an upcoming women's retreat. I bounced my thoughts off Patty, "Who knew that I would be good at that? Who can I be for church?"

When we arrived home, l went straight to the bookcase and pulled out my copy of *Each New Day*. It was worn and yellowing with age. I looked into the peaceful eyes of my friend. "I'll be Corrie ten Boom!" I announced confidently to Patty. She flashed me a look, because I had already committed to teaching two other classes. We were both trying to learn where God was working in our lives and cooperate. My ideas were a little "out there" for Patty but, she was supportive.

My thoughts encouraged me. *Corrie has helped me with my problems. I already feel like I know her. I love playing an old woman. The costume can be used for her, with just a few changes.*

I had recently read *In my Father's House*, where Corrie explained how God had prepared her from childhood to do the things she did when she was old. It was encouraging to me to think about God being at work on his plan all along. I thought the ladies at my church would love to hear the story. It was a natural step from volunteer work at the museum to volunteer work at my church. It seemed right.

When I think back to my night of surrender to the Lord, I gave him everything. I had not acted in years, and never thought I would have an occasion to act again. I was not sad over that. I just thought that acting was the old life, and I was moving onto a new life. I had given it up, but God gave it back to me. I needed to be available and willing.

My mother taught me to love and respect older women. She did it not by words, but by her actions. I loved the old Corrie. I appreciated the old Laura Clubb. I loved Mama and her quiet wisdom, and she is the reason I loved being an old woman. She helped build my character and gave me a critical item of my costume. God was at work weaving his plan all along in me.

The Weaving

Sensible Shoes

In the book, *The Hiding Place*, John and Elizabeth Sherrill described Corrie as a woman "sensible of shoe." To me that meant comfort- and utility-driven shoe choices. I had a certain respect for those choices, especially as I got older. In some cases, I thought sensible also meant ugly. Corrie's attitude about her appearance as well as her shoes spoke volumes to me. She wrote that she was never as careful of her appearance as her sisters were.

Frequently my audience asks, "Where did you get those shoes?" It is asked with an incredulous tone, signifying that the inquirer can hardly believe such worn, utilitarian shoes from years past would have been saved. I grin at the implication of the question, and answer truthfully with a believe-it-or-not tone, "In my mother's closet."

Like Corrie, my mother was similarly unimpressed with clothes, style, or trends. Mama was motivated by her main desire to be comfortable. Since back surgery in 1959 when she was in her thirties,

Mama decided to wear the most utilitarian oxfords she could find. They were ugly to us kids. You could not buy shoes that unattractive just anywhere at that time—there were only certain stores that carried them or could order them. They had a sturdy, thick heel several inches high. Mama defended the ugly shoes by explaining the doctor said she had to have a heel on her shoe. Therefore, she wore those shoes all the time. In summer she had a white pair and in winter a new black pair. Mama rarely wore any other shoes because, according to her, others would "…just kill my back." It was somewhat embarrassing for us kids to have such an old-fashioned mother, but we loved her and enjoyed kidding her about it. Of course, efforts to try to change her were like butting our heads against the wall. She wore those ugly shoes for years.

I like shoes, as most women do. Shoes have long been one of the most defining components of my wardrobe. You can say a lot with a pair of shoes. I have learned you can dress any outfit up or down with the right shoes. When I was collecting the costume for an old woman from the 1950s, I thought about how important the shoes would be to accomplish that. Then I remembered Mama's old black shoes. Because Mama was a saver, I would not have been surprised to find she kept a pair of her ugly shoes for hard times. I dialed the long distance number that I called nearly every day to hear my Mama's voice. She loves to help people, so I posed my question as a need, "Where are those old black shoes you used to wear? I need them for a costume." I knew she might not give them to me, if she did not think I really needed them. She knew right where her old shoes were stored and was happy to help.

I made a trip to Kansas City to get Mama's old shoes. They had been in the bottom of her cluttered closet. Mama enjoys fixing old things to make them useful again, so she polished the shoes and gave them new strings so they, according to her, "would not look so bad."

When I tried the shoes on, they were a little big. So, I needed to stuff the toes and tie the laces tightly. We laughed together about how funny I looked in my contemporary clothes with those old-lady shoes. It reminded us of the time when I came home from college in 1967 to find and resurrect a vintage woolen military shirt to wear with my jeans and tee shirts. Mama was accustomed to her children doing things that she thought were strange. After all, she had seven children and the first four were teenagers in the '60s, so her shock level had already been tested way back then. I smiled, thinking some things never change. She was as amused as I was, and thankful that her old shoes would be perfect for my costume.

I wore Mama's shoes for my Laura Clubb presentation, and when I was getting my costume for Corrie together, I knew they would be perfect. However, the vintage navy party dress needed some help. Old ladies sometimes put sweaters over their dresses, so I looked in my stash of sweaters at home. I found an old navy wool sweater that I thought would work. The different shades of navy never quite match and these were no exception, but I liked the idea of a slight mismatch.

Later in my research, I found a description of an outfit Corrie had assembled for herself and worn before her young traveling companion could object. She had on three shades of blue and none matched. I laughed to myself as I believed God had even delighted me by the details because my costume was the same color as what I read about in the book. Corrie's lack of fashion sense reminded me of my mother in that I often felt like she needed me to be her fashion police.

My interest in art, a pioneer woman, acting, teaching, costumes, and shoes were all used to prepare me to take the stage as Corrie. I sometimes meet people who actually knew or saw Corrie when she was in the United States and speaking in the 1970s. Several times I have heard, "Those are just like the shoes she wore." I smile and think about how God weaves our lives. He prepares us and gives us what we need before we even know to ask. I believe God is in the details—my mother, her attitudes that shaped me, a navy dress, and even sensible shoes.

Mama's sensible shoes

Corrie's Hanky Story

From *Corrie ten Boom Live*:

One day in the barracks, I thought "Today, I cannot stand it." I had caught a cold and my nose was running. I had nothing to wipe my nose. I had only my thin prison dress on.

I complained to my sister and she said, "We shall pray. Dear God, please send Corrie a hanky for she has caught a cold. Amen."

I laughed. Of all the need in that camp and in the world that Betsie would ask for me to get a hanky. How impossible it was anyway. There were no hankies for prisoners.

But, in a few minutes I heard a knock at the window beside me. It was my friend, a fellow prisoner. I asked, "Have you come for a visit?"

She said, "No, no. I have something for you." She passed to me a small package and inside was a hanky!

I said, "Why, did you bring me this?"

She said, "I was in the prison hospital, working. I found an old sheet and I was making hankies from the old sheet, and something in my heart said take a hanky to Corrie ten Boom."

Do you know what a hanky can tell you at a time like that? That hanky told me that there was a God who cared. He heard an impossible prayer from one of His suffering old servants, and He put it in the heart of another servant to meet that need. That is the foolishness of God. But the foolishness of God is wiser than man's wisdom. Nothing is too small for His love!

I delivered Corrie's line with a booming voice, "Do you know what a hanky can tell you at a time like this?" I often had to pause momentarily to regain my composure. It brought me to tears, as I got a fresh sense of awe at God's love and mercy that he lets us know without a doubt that he hears our prayers.

Corrie was a natural born teacher and made great use of visual aids. The story of her small need of a hanky that God answered encourages me to pray and expect to see answers—even in the smallest things.

It was just days before my first performance as Corrie that a woman from my church that I did not know well approached me. She had in her hand an audio tape of one of Corrie's talks. She explained that she was going through her grandmother's things and found the tape in a box. She said she wondered if I would like to have it. Needless to say, it was a hanky moment for me. I had just prayed for help, and received a tape of Corrie's speech and her voice to study *just in time*. That tape told me he had directed me to this work and knew what I needed.

Corrie wrote that she and her father often prayed over their work in the watch shop during the twenty-five years they worked together. When they encountered a problem in a watch they had difficulty with, they would pray for God to show them how to fix it. She reported that miraculously they would later be directed to the solution.

I could relate to that miracle. I thought back to the time when I worked as an airline mechanic. It was the hardest job I ever had. I never had any interest in or uncanny ability in the skills I needed for that job. I often wondered how I could make it through each day. I had to pray to God for some of the smallest, but impossible things. I remember praying that I could get a simple screw inserted correctly. I felt that often God encouraged me by answering those cries in miraculous ways. I took my faith as literally as Corrie did. I figured Savior meant saving me from daily dilemmas too.

When Corrie laughed that Betsie would pray for God to give her a hanky, she might have been reminded of her father and the watch shop. I wondered if she allowed herself to forget God's miracles long enough to get discouraged sometimes. In the concentration camp, Betsie was often the one to encourage Corrie to keep her eyes on God instead of her circumstances.

Sometimes I find myself drifting from God and depending on myself to solve my problems, and that is when I become discouraged. Corrie reminds me with her hanky story to pray about everything. Nothing is too small for his love. There is a lot of encouragement when you know in your heart of hearts that God heard your impossible request and provided a way for you. It is when I think about the details that I become more confident to pray about everything.

I seek to apply the hanky principle every day in my life. God hears and cares about even the smallest things. All the threads in the weaving of our lives are crucial, and they are in his hands. To me, that is very good news! I would soon see a bright thread emerge in answer to prayer.

Vision

Since my first performance I have had answers to prayer for small things, but also for big things. My ministry has developed slowly by word of mouth. I felt strongly that I needed to know that God was behind each step. I did not have a vision where he was leading me, but I enjoyed performing, and I wanted to be prepared to teach also. After my first performance as Corrie, I began to take training from Florence Littauer and her team at CLASS (Christian Leaders and Speakers Seminars).

The conferences were a lot of fun because Florence is not only a gifted speaker and teacher, but she is also very funny. I loved hearing her stories, as well as hearing stories from other women I met there. Almost all of them had some tragedy and heartache in their lives they had overcome. Their stories illustrated the same principle behind Corrie's weaving poem. Dark and bright threads are part of God's plan.

One day in 1999, I received a schedule of upcoming CLASS seminars. I could hardly believe my eyes when I read that Florence was offering a mentoring session at her home in California for six people! I knew she had a busy speaking schedule, in addition to teaching, and I did not know anyone around that was better. Florence started teaching speech and drama right out of college and had years of experience. I studied video tapes of her to learn more about her teaching on the personalities, and also to study her teaching style.

After reading the news of her mentoring session, I began to pray, "Oh, Lord, help me be able to go to this." I did not ask my husband or wait to think about it. I just grabbed the phone and called the mentoring session number. I got no answer and no answering machine. I kept trying a few more times. Still, there was no answer. I was frustrated and afraid the class would fill up before I could get signed up.

I do not know how God did it, but mercifully I got busy on something else and forgot all about the mentoring session until the following Monday. I dialed the number, and Fred Littauer answered cheerfully. I told him I would like to attend the January group. "Oh, that's the one that's most available," he said. I was elated!

I rattled on to Fred about how much I learned from Florence's books and classes. He said, "She's right here, having breakfast. You can tell her." I do not know what I said to Florence. I could hardly believe I was talking with her.

After I got off the phone, I was bouncing off the walls and could not wait to tell Rob. When I settled down a little and read all the particulars, I realized each attendee would speak for thirty minutes in front of Florence, the master. I began to think about that. *Heavens, you are bold, but what on earth do you think you will you do in front of Florence?* I relaxed as I realized I could just do *Corrie.* I taught and spoke on several subjects, but I would be pretty intimidated to stand in front of Florence and teach. When I acted, it was not me, so in my mind that would be easier.

In January of 2000, I had the incredible opportunity to attend a session of Upper CLASS, the mentoring session. I flew to California and Fred picked me up at the airport. There were six of us from all over the country. It was decided that I should go first in the group. I had the 9:00 A.M. slot for my performance in Florence's living room. I was staying in a condo a few doors away. I dressed in my costume and walked down to our meeting. Florence and our small group of women speakers were seated in a semi-circle in the living room. I was relaxed as I gave my performance with the confidence that God had sent me there for a reason.

Afterwards, one woman grabbed the Kleenex box and passed tissues around. There were tears. Each woman took a turn expressing her reaction. It was all positive feedback, but one comment touched my heart. One of my roommates said, "I can see why God has had you so alone and isolated." That blessed me because I had shared with her that I often felt isolated in Oklahoma. There was time to read and think in the long evening hours alone while my husband worked, but maybe that situation had been good for me.

Florence did not say a word until the others finished. What could anyone say after she spoke anyway? I heard, "I almost don't know what to say to you." My stomach felt like it took a hard punch. I thought, *She thinks you need so much work, she doesn't even know where to start.* I had expected some drama tips since Florence had a background in theater. I wanted the floor to open up and swallow me. My mind raced. *How can I get out of here?*

A few seconds passed and Florence continued with, "You are so overwhelming and so powerful, that I don't know what to say." She said she was glad she had a tissue stuffed in her pocket, "I thought of people I knew during the war." When I asked for her dramatic direction, she advised, "I wouldn't touch a thing."

I must have floated back to my room to change out of my costume. It would be months before I came down from that high—even a little. I had a lot of respect for Florence, and her comments and encouragement meant a lot to me. Could it be true? Was God really going to use me in this way?

I was on the mountaintop for quite awhile after the time with Florence, and I cherished the memory. But I have had quite a bit of time in the valley since. Mentor Fred Smith says the mountaintop is the time to get the vision but you grow the food you need in the valley. It is the same principle as *The Weaving*. Both the good times and the bad times are part of the package of God's plans. In Florence's living room, I received the vision to expand my ministry.

Evelyn with Florence Littauer
at her home in California.

Go to All the World

I remember an evening in Oklahoma when I picked up my Bible, and this verse jumped off the page:

You must go to everyone I send you to and say whatever I command you. Do not be afraid of them, for I am with you and will rescue you. Jeremiah 1:7-8 NIV

I got goosebumps as I felt God speaking to me. It was scary and exciting at the same time. I knew I could be fearless and confident one minute, and shaking inside with fears and doubts the next. I did not know where God would send me but I *knew* I heard the call.

The vision for my ministry expanded from the moment I heard Florence Littauer's encouragement. One of my roommates from the seminar, Judy Bragg, told the Bible study she attended in Dallas about me. I received an invitation to perform there on Easter in

2000. I was "going" out from Oklahoma to Texas. It was a big step.

In addition, my life at home was in transition. Rob and I had been considering moving for more than a year, as we wondered if we should move just to a different house or transfer to Dallas. Rob tested the waters that spring by submitting a transfer at his job. We were both surprised when a new position in Dallas opened up in just two short weeks. We felt like God was behind it. I was particularly happy to be moving to a larger city, and excited with the possibilities that God was going to use me.

About all I knew about Judy's group in Dallas was that it was not a church. It was a Bible study and met every Sunday just like a church—but in a country club. I had never heard of a group like that, but I figured maybe that was the way things were done in big "D." I had visited Dallas before, but did not really know that much about it.

On the Sunday I was to perform, the Bent Tree Bible Study was meeting at the Hotel Intercontinental. The lobby was impressive with its polished marble and flower arrangements. The group met in a ballroom, and I checked it out as soon as I arrived. It was set up with round tables with white tablecloths for about one hundred people. I was to perform on the skirted platform at the front. A small table was set there for me to use. That was all perfect for what I needed.

At the back of the room there were tables with coffee and a continental breakfast. People were beginning to filter in, getting their coffee and filling up the tables in the room. They were well dressed, and I could tell that this group was an upscale kind of group. I enjoyed noticing there were a few Easter hats too.

I had been warmly greeted at the door by a man I would later learn was the official greeter, John Talley. I stayed by the entrance a few minutes, and the leader, Garry Kinder, came in with his wife Janet behind him. I gave him a friendly Oklahoma greeting, "It's nice to meet you, preacher."

Garry quickly and firmly corrected me with no elaboration, "I am not a preacher," as he went on into the ballroom.

I was a bit embarrassed at my mistake. I was beginning to see that I had a lot to learn. I went to the elegant ladies' room to change into my costume. Second thoughts began to fill me with fear. My insides were churning. *Who are these people and will they even care about Corrie ten Boom?* Quickly, I had to stop and pray. *Yes Lord, you've called me. Your Spirit will do the work through me.*

I calmed down enough to get into my costume. My nervous hurrying made my padding bunch up and every step seemed to be extra difficult, but I kept at it. I went to the mirror to get my wig, hat, and glasses on just right. I was hoping no one would come into the restroom, so I would not need to make any explanations. When I was ready, I walked down the hall and slipped into the back of the ballroom and sat in the chair reserved for me.

Garry Kinder was in the back of the room also, and Donna Skell was at the front taking prayer requests. Garry came over and patted my shoulder in a friendly way. It was to encourage me, I was sure. However, as I thought about it, he seemed to just be welcoming a rather old lady visiting the class. *That's good. This costume is so believable that there is nothing of me showing.*

I was nervous when I walked up the side of the room to get to the platform while I was being introduced. After I began my performance though, I began to relax as I became a confident Corrie. The crowd of well-dressed ladies and men and a few children were very responsive. I was glad when they laughed a few times. When I finished, they stood to give me a standing ovation!

Garry took command of the microphone after I had taken my bows. He had not heard the presentation before, but he focused on elements of the message and repeated them several times to his class. I went to the back of the room and listened. I was impressed with the way Garry led the group, and also thankful and happy that they seemed to get the message.

Afterwards, the people lined up to greet and thank me. They seemed genuinely appreciative of Corrie's message, and I felt a warm welcome. I was impressed with the sincerity I heard earlier in Garry's voice when he said, "We are a praying class." Before leaving, I asked Executive Director, John Gillespie, to pray for me and my husband's move to Dallas, and for my ministry.

Within a few weeks my husband and I moved to Dallas, and Rob started work on the night shift. That meant he slept on Sunday mornings. We found a church with a Saturday night service that we could go to together. But, I had no place to be on Sunday morning. If I stayed home, I had to be quiet and I wanted to get out. I was used to going to church on Sundays. I decided to see if I could find the country club where Bent Tree Bible Study met. I did not know many people in Dallas, but I felt like I knew a few at the Bible study after being with them once.

It was raining on the Sunday morning I set out with very poor instructions. I had a lot to learn about Dallas and clear directions was one of them. I found the intersection of Arapaho and Preston, but did not see Prestonwood Country Club. I drove up, down and around Arapaho—even stopping a jogger for directions. The jogger was clueless. Mercifully, I finally spotted the entrance off Preston and drove in and parked. I was late by then and it was raining, but the option of turning around and driving home did not sound good.

I met Steve and Laverne Bialas on my way in the door that Sunday morning, and they welcomed me when I told them I had played Corrie. I joined the group and sat at a table in the back. Garry taught an excellent Bible lesson. Janet Kinder slid a piece of paper over to me with her phone number, and told me to call her sometime for lunch. Great teaching, friendly people, and a beautiful setting— that was what I found at the Bible study and it drew me in. It made the decision to be a regular member pretty easy.

I do not always get feedback about how my performance impacted people. I performed and then left. Since I attended the Bible study group, I got to hear some of how my performance affected people. Jim and Connie Tolbert told me their five-year-old granddaughter identified with Corrie. She later asked Jesus into her heart like Corrie had at age five. The young girl continued to grow and to love Jesus as well as Corrie. An elderly member of the class, Mrs. Newell, especially enjoyed the performance. She was convinced it was the real Corrie who had visited the class and would not be persuaded otherwise.

Today, our group is known as Roaring Lambs Bible Study. Garry Kinder faithfully teaches each week. One of my favorite expressions of his is "The Bible is all about 'Go!'" Everyone is called to go and tell. I followed in obedience to Dallas and was soon called to go further.

Evelyn and Rob with Garry and Janet Kinder
at the Roaring Lambs Bible Study

The Beje

"I've been there," many people tell me after my performance. They are proud of the fact that not only do they know about Corrie, but also they have visited her home in Holland, the Beje. I felt as if I had been there from reading books and watching films, but there really is not anything like the actual experience. I had wanted to go for a long time and prayed that the right time—God's time—would come.

I remember when the phone rang at my home in Oklahoma before my very first performance as Corrie. It was a woman from my church with a question, "It can't be Corrie ten Boom coming to our ladies' retreat. Is it her companion?"

I laughed as I explained, "No, it's me." Then we both laughed. This woman worked at a church in Tulsa, and she had proudly told them that Corrie was coming to her church in Claremore. Her co-workers had set her straight—it could not be Corrie because she was dead.

They told her that our church's guest speaker probably was Pam Rosewell Moore, Corrie's traveling companion. Then it was my time to be confused because I did not know about Pam. However, I was thrilled with the possibility of more resources about Corrie.

In 1997 I was given the number for Pam and phoned her at Dallas Baptist University. Weeks later, she returned my call. I had a short phone interview with this English woman who traveled with "Tante" Corrie in her final years, and stayed with her through her illness and death. I learned that Pam wrote about those years in her book, *The Five Silent Years of Corrie ten Boom*. She told me that DBU had a Corrie ten Boom memorial room in the library, and that I could visit. "Many people pass through Dallas and visit," she said. I told her I would like to do that, and she made a point of saying I should contact her when I came. It was not long before Rob came home from work with the announcement, "I'm going to Dallas for a week of training." I saw it as a sign from God that it was my opportunity to visit Corrie's room.

On the day I visited, I was able to listen to Pam speak to a school group about her experiences with Corrie. I visited the memorial room where there was a table, chairs, and cabinets with some of Corrie's possessions behind glass. There were photos and a painting on the walls. Pam told me that sometimes the staff found people in the room weeping. From her, I learned more about the anointing that was on Corrie's life.

After my husband and I moved to Dallas in 2000, I made my second visit to Corrie's memorial room. While I was there, I visited Pam again in her office. I am afraid I babbled in my excitement over my ministry, and went on that I wanted to go to Holland to visit the Beje. *Ask her if she would like to go.* I argued with the voice I heard inside me. *I can't do that. She hardly knows me.* Almost immediately,

I heard again, *Ask if she wants to go.* This time, I simply blurted out, "You wouldn't want to go too, would you?" I shocked myself with my boldness. Pam seemed to have a reserved personality, and I had the impression that I was a little over the top for her.

"Actually, I've been thinking of going," was Pam's astounding answer. I left that day with the idea that Pam would pray about it, and let me know. I felt like I was living in a dream as I drove the thirty-minute trip home that day. Not only did I get to meet Pam and talk with her, but I might get to visit Holland with her! A few days later Pam called my home and told me she decided to make the trip, and I could travel with her. Over the next few days, she checked her schedule and arrangements with her friends in Holland, and set the dates to travel in December of 2000.

I had several months to anticipate this over-the-top answer to my prayer for a time to visit Corrie's home. My anticipation of the trip and my assurance that only God could have arranged it was a huge part of my excitement.

Florence Littauer encouraged me to take pictures of myself in costume at the Beje. I explained to Pam that I would be taking my costume to do that. She told me she would be speaking to several groups while we were in Holland. I summoned my courage and boldly offered that I would like to present my Corrie if there was an opportunity.

That opportunity came on December 11, 2000. Frits Nieuwstraten, managing director of the Beje, invited Pam and me to attend the Christmas party for the Beje's volunteer tour guides. Pam told him that I wanted to perform, and he agreed. Not only did I get to visit her home and country, but also I was allowed to present my Corrie in her home.

On the evening of the party, Pam and I walked the few blocks from our hotel to the Beje. I asked where I could change into my costume, and they took me to Corrie's bedroom. They found a mirror and carried it up the stairs to the room for me to use. As I climbed those narrow winding stairs to Corrie's bedroom, I had goosebumps. The room was chilly, but I felt almost feverish as I struggled to put my costume on and get the padding in the right places. I checked my wig and dress in the mirror before I left the room.

I had given myself fifteen minutes to dress, but I was ready early. I was nervous and excited and felt a little too warm in my costume with all the padding. I spent a few moments to collect my thoughts and silently thank God for the opportunity. I passed by the small bathroom outside Corrie's bedroom door, and slowly descended the stairs to what is now called the "Liberation Room." It is the living room directly above the watch shop.

I remembered that I read about how Father ten Boom had everyone gather in that room in the evening. They used that room to entertain many visitors. In that room, the Beje had classes, concerts, and even plays. Now, I was there to do my play.

Nineteen people were present that evening, sitting in a circle around the room. There was a festive glow there, warmed by what the Dutch call "gezellig," a coziness and hospitality they are known for. The volunteers were talkative and seemed to be in a holiday mood.

I entered the room in character and gave a short message as Corrie. I hardly knew what I was saying because of my excitement. It was definitely an out-of-body experience.

Visiting the Beje, and being able to stand in the hiding place behind the wall in Corrie's room was a long-time ambition fulfilled for me. Visiting there with Pam Moore and performing in the living room was so much more than I had asked for or could imagine. I was reminded of this Bible verse:

Now unto Him that is able to do exceeding abundantly beyond all that we ask or think, according to the power that works within us. Ephesians 3:20 NASB

I was learning that God could do more than I could imagine, as I learned more about Corrie and her work.

Evelyn performing at the Beje in Holland in 2000.

Evelyn standing in Corrie's bedroom in front of the hiding place.

The Weaving

A House for Corrie's Work

One of the cold December days we were in Holland, Beje tour guide Betty Veldhuijzenvan Zanten and her husband picked Pam and me up from our hotel for an outing to visit a home that Corrie used in her work after the war. Pam speaks Dutch so they were visiting while I looked out at the scenery while we drove from Haarlem to Bloemendaal. We drove down a path in a wooded area that led us to a grand-looking home on what I assumed was a very large, somewhat overgrown yard. Betty knocked on the door to see if anyone was home. A young woman answered and they spoke in Dutch. I was told that a young couple lived there with their two small children and a brother-in-law. We were invited in, and I stood in the foyer while the others talked.

It appeared that some of the rooms were closed off. I imagined that was to conserve heating costs. There was intricately carved woodwork on the staircase. I had seen it in a film about Corrie, but now I was here in person. For a moment, I flashed back to Betsie ten Boom's description and vision. Sometime before her death in Ravensbruck, Betsie began to think of the needs of the people after the war ended. She had a vision to minister to people hurting after the war. She described to Corrie a house that they would use to minister to those people. Betsie described details in the house as if God had shown it to her, especially the beautiful woodwork in the home.

After the war, Corrie fulfilled Betsie's vision. A woman heard of Corrie's work and offered her large home to be used to house people in need. I was standing in the very home I had read about it. When Corrie visited the home the first time, she commented on the woodwork. The owner was surprised and asked if she had seen it before, and she responded that in some way she *had* seen it. She had seen it as Betsie had painted it with her words.

It is a moment frozen in my memory now. God gave the vision of the work to be done to Betsie, and Corrie lived it out. For a moment, I felt like I was part of it by being there. Betsie told Corrie, "Everything that happens to us is a preparation for the work we will do next." While Betsie lay dying in Barracks Twenty-Eight in the Ravensbruck concentration camp, she was praying and seeking how she could serve God after her release. Her faith and encouragement helped prepare Corrie for her work after the war.

The trip to Holland helped me to understand more about Corrie's work. Everything I learned about her gave me more respect for all she accomplished. Corrie was ordinary, but she did extraordinary work because of her faith. I thought, *Corrie's God is my God. What work lies ahead for me? What are these threads of experience preparing me for?*

*Betty, Pam, and Evelyn in front of
Schapenduinen home in Holland.*

The Weaving

Writing Books

Florence Littauer said to me firmly, "You've got a book in you, and we need to get it out." I was surprised, but I believed it because of the conviction in her voice. I had a lot of respect for her opinions. We were sitting at the dinner table in her home with others attending the Upper CLASS seminar. Later, Florence advised me to begin writing my book even if no one but my family ever read it. I thought it was good advice, and the Lord directing me through her counsel.

I never thought about writing a book before Florence suggested it. I loved to read and words were my passion since I learned to read as a child. I graduated with honors in my major, English Language and Literature. Still, memories of agonizing over each word on papers for school were not very pleasant. My perfectionistic thoughts bedeviled me. *What do I want to say? There are a million ways to tell my story. What is the right way?*

I would rather talk than write. At least while talking, I get facial and verbal clues when people are not following what I am saying. To help me communicate, I use facial expressions and my voice. It is so much easier for me to talk than write that I did not look forward to writing. Still, I wanted to be obedient to the Lord, and I began to write. It was not easy for me, and I had a million excuses. I thought a lot about Corrie and her writing.

When Corrie arrived back in Holland after her release from Ravensbruck concentration camp, she found her home ransacked. I tried to imagine how she felt. Everything was different. The watch shop was no longer alive with the presence of her old father. As she walked through the rooms of the Beje that had been the home of the Ten Boom family for more than 100 years, I can only guess what thoughts went through her mind. The home was no longer filled with the voices of family and friends.

Corrie had suffered many losses. Father ten Boom died in prison, Corrie's sister and mentor Betsie had died, her brother Willem was a sick man when he was released from prison and died from his illness shortly afterward, and her nephew Kik remained missing. Hope of his return soon faded. It was not until 1953 that the family learned he had died in the concentration camp of Bergen-Belsen in 1944.

In 1945 Corrie was weak and still sick from her imprisonment. After spending some time recovering in a hospital, I imagine she began to sort through the pain and grief to find God's plan. She wrote that she continued to wake up in the early hours of the morning, just as she had in the concentration camp. I wondered, *How did she keep from being crippled with depression?*

It was at this time that Corrie began to write her first book, *A Prisoner and Yet*. She wrote the story while it was still fresh in her mind. Evidently, many Dutch people wanted to know what happened in the camps, and her book became a bestseller. Corrie was experienced at teaching and storytelling. She had been trained by her family to see God's hand in everything and began to tell her story in print from the point of victory.

Corrie wrote that the Beje had a wooden plaque that read "Jesus is overwinnar" (Jesus is Victor.) Those three words summed up what the Ten Boom family stood for. She took the saying for her life.

As I began to write, I wondered about Corrie's courage and tenacity. *How much opposition did she encounter from the enemy? Did well-meaning friends tell her to "put those bad memories behind" and "don't put yourself through the pain of writing the story?" Did she wonder about her ability to write a book?* Most of her work had been in front of small groups teaching—not sitting in a silent room writing.

I read what Corrie wrote in *The Hiding Place*:

In churches and club rooms and private homes in those desperate days (in 1945), I told the truths Betsie and I had learned in Ravensbruck.

Words are words, I suppose, and Corrie was trained to use words in her teaching. Somehow, she put together the story in writing. It was first published in Holland in 1946 while the market was hungry for stories from the war.

Corrie could not have known the impact that the book would have. Thankfully, she was simply obedient to the task at hand. I wondered,

Did the words come easily at first and was it healing to write? Certainly, the entire process could not have been without pain and thoughts of failure. My thoughts continued, *How many times did she want to give up? How did God's hand guide her through it and guide people to help her?* To me, part of the value of her first book is that it came from her heart while her experiences were still fresh. She did not have much time to heal or put a historical perspective on what happened. It was the beginning of a writing career that would span the next thirty years.

I did not learn about *A Prisoner and Yet* until 1997 when Pam Moore told me about it. What a treat it was to read Corrie's first published account of her days in prison. I felt as if I had found buried treasure, and I knew God was leading me to more resources that would broaden my knowledge, helping me to portray Corrie.

In 2000 on my trip to Holland, I held in my hands a copy of a first edition of *A Prisoner and Yet.* I had just given a performance at Holland's YWAM ministry and was visiting their library that is named for Corrie. The book had an illustration of the women in the bunks of the camp. Those bunks seemed hardly more than shelves. My heart was touched again by the suffering she endured. As my fingers turned the pages, I wondered how many Dutch people had read that copy of the book, and how it impacted them. I also wondered how she found a publisher and wrote it so quickly.

As I sat in my comfortable office chair in front of the computer in my pleasant home office, I was immersed in the writing of my first book. I thought, *Writing is so solitary and takes so much time. Do I even have enough hours left on earth to finish a book? Will anyone care enough to read it?*

Once again Corrie's courage inspired me. She might have had to write by the light of a kerosene lamp because much of Holland was without electricity at the end of the war. Corrie did not have all the computer and office aids that I do. She also had an ancient old home and shop to take care of. I had a new modern home in a convenient American metroplex. My obstacles and excuses paled in comparison. God prepared her and she wrote. If God provided a way for Corrie, he would provide a way for me. I just needed to be available and obedient.

The Weaving

A Thread By the Grave

"You can't leave without seeing it!" Armene settled the issue in a firm tone, and all of a sudden my afternoon activities were changed by a relative stranger. We were discussing Corrie's gravesite. It was July, 2002 and I was attending a CLASS conference held in conjunction with the Christian Booksellers Convention in Anaheim, California.

I was in a group of women sitting at one of the round tables that crowded the banquet room of a hotel near the convention center. It was lunch time, and the table was full. We did not know each other, so we took turns telling about our speaking ministry or book. I simply offered, "I am an actress and a speaker, and I portray Corrie ten Boom." Two women across the table lit up and began to tell what they knew about Corrie. I learned that these women lived in the area, and had seen Corrie and knew others that knew her.

Armene said, "You know, she's buried near here." I remembered reading that Corrie was buried in Orange County. I had not made that connection before. I thought many times that I would like to have the opportunity to visit her grave, the same way I might visit my grandmother's, to pay tribute to her memory. Many arrangements would have to be made to fly there, get a car, hotel, and directions. So, I just filed it away in my mind as a project to do someday.

I was struggling with some health issues, and attending the conference was an act of faith. I was feeling weak and tired, and just trying to make it through the day. My answer sounded as weak as I felt, "I would like to visit it someday."

When Armene learned that I lived in Texas, she boldly took charge, "You can't leave without seeing it—you are so close." She and several other local Californians sprang into action to discuss how I could visit Corrie's grave.

As we finished our lunch, I was amused at the coincidences. *How did we end up together at that particular table? Why were my tablemates so determined about my afternoon plans? God is always providing me with surprises.*

While my acquaintances at the California conference saw the solution, I saw the problems. I thought, *I am not dressed for walking around in a cemetery. How do I get there without a car? Will I be able to find it?*

Armene took charge and took me to her car in the hotel parking lot. She found her map book in the trunk, and located the page that showed the cemetery, putting it into my hands. Armene called directory assistance on her cell phone and got the number of the cemetery. She dialed the office and explained the situation, "I am with Evelyn Hinds, and she portrays Corrie ten Boom. She would like to visit Corrie's grave. She will be coming in a cab. Would you direct her to the grave? She will be there shortly."

I said goodbye to my new acquaintance Armene as she headed to the convention center for her next appointment. In the lobby, I asked the doorman to flag a taxi. I was uneasy and wondered if a cab would wait for me. Anxious thoughts crowded my head. *How long will it take to find the grave? What will the trip cost?* I tried to explain what I needed to the cab driver. He was a new emigrant from China, and did not seem to understand English well. I pointed at the map a lot. I do not know if he understood the map, but he pulled it out of my hands and put it in the front seat beside him. He nodded with a no-problem attitude.

I sat in the back seat, but tried to offer my help driving. I read the road signs out loud when the driver appeared confused about which direction to go. I was relieved when I finally saw the sign for the cemetery. My young cabdriver parked the taxi at the administration building just inside the entrance. He nodded agreeably that he would wait for me.

I hurried inside the building and found the receptionist. She had taken the earlier call from Armene. She was eager to tell me how she loved Corrie, and especially Betsie, from reading Corrie's books. She was not surprised by my visit, "We have a lot of visitors to her grave."

The friendly receptionist called another woman, and she came out with a map to direct me to the grave. It looked like an incomprehensible maze to me. The property had many acres of graves. I asked her if she would point me to the grave. We stepped outside, and she pointed to a section behind the administration building not too far away. She told me to count in a certain number of rows from the curb. I thought that sounded simple enough, thanked her, and set out walking.

Arriving at what I thought was the appropriate curb, I counted in the number of rows. I had not seen any sign indicating that it was Lawn A as the map showed. The headstones were all level with the carpet of grass. I was watching each step I took and was glad I had put on my flat Mary Jane shoes. At the appropriate row I did not see any marker for Corrie ten Boom. Second guessing my understanding of the directions, I wondered if the woman meant for me to count from the other curb. So I tried that. Still, the headstone was not there. I headed back to the street to ask someone else to clarify the directions. There was no one to ask. I waited until a workman passed me in a truck, but evidently he did not see me signal him to stop.

I was getting overheated in my black jacket in the hot California sun. I felt like I needed to hurry back to the cab. I prayed for God to help. I spoke to Corrie in my heart, *At least I'm close. I love you and want to honor you.* I tried again to count the rows in neatly manicured Lawn A. I walked a few steps this way and that way, and turned around a few times. Just as I was ready to give up, there it was! The marker simply read: Jesus is Victor, Corrie ten Boom, 1892-1983.

I knelt in gratitude. I knew this was a historic moment for me, and I wanted to remember it. There was a vase buried in the grass. It held two flowers in water. The flowers were faded, but were evidence that someone had visited the grave only a day or two before me. I wondered who that person was, and how Corrie ten Boom had impacted them.

I got up and walked quickly back towards the administration building. I wondered how Corrie, an ordinary Dutch woman, had ended up in such a prominent place in this beautiful cemetery. It was a long way from Haarlem.

I was glad to get back to the taxi. I was quiet all the way back to the hotel and I imagined my young driver was thankful for that. I was lost in my thoughts about all the pieces that had to fall into place for this visit to happen. My body was weak, but God knew I wanted to visit the grave and he paired me up with someone assertive enough to make it happen. It was another example to me that all I needed to do was show up, be available, and be willing.

The Weaving

God's Timing

"You can't let fear control your life!" Rob challenged me. He made plans to go to India for some training, but it really was not on my list of places to go. I knew instantly that he was right—it was only fear holding me back. Conflicting thoughts ran through my head. *I don't want to go. I'm afraid. How often do I get an opportunity to travel to India? I do enjoy traveling.* I uttered my weak resolve, "OK, I'll go."

Rob and I often talked about how fear held us back, and we tried to recognize it and root it out. In *Tramp for the Lord*, Corrie impressed me with her fearlessness. I thought, *After being in a concentration camp, what would scare you?* I hoped I never had to find that out. Still, I thought about when I worked as an airline mechanic. I did not know how I survived—except that God was with me. When I thought back to those days, it gave me courage that the same God was with me now. I could not let fear hold me back!

I knew that Corrie had traveled in India during her ministry. I was always looking for opportunities to perform, but I was disappointed when a potential contact for India fell through. I am often painfully aware that it has to be God's timing—not mine.

The Saturday before my India trip, I went to a group meeting that Rob and I usually attended together. Rob had been in India for a week already. Our meeting was with a well-known Christian mentor, Fred Smith. Fred is a man disabled in body, but strong in mind and spirit. At age ninety he is still helping people with his wisdom and insight. The meeting took place in the Dallas home of his daughter Brenda Smith. Fred's large bedroom was set up with chairs around his bed.

I noticed that Dr. Ramesh Richard joined the group after we had started. He was a professor at Dallas Theological Seminary, as well as an international teacher and author (www.rreach.org). I had heard about Dr. Richard from Fred and looked at his website, enjoyed his writing, and wanted to meet him. He was originally from India, and I was scheduled to leave for India in six days.

When the meeting ended, I navigated my way through the crowd in the bedroom in order to meet Dr. Richard. I told him I was leaving for India in a few days and had a card of my ministry to give him. He immediately told me that Corrie ten Boom had visited their home when he was a child. He asked me where I was going in India, and I explained that my husband was in New Delhi. Dr. Richard replied quickly, "I used to be a pastor in New Delhi, and I have a friend who is a pastor there. They would love to see your presentation."

Dr. Richard introduced me to his father who had accompanied him to the meeting that morning. Dr. John Richard is a minister-at-large for a missionary group. He told me about the time he was with Corrie in India. He was assigned to be her escort and take her to meetings. She asked to meet his wife, but Dr. Richard explained that she was at home with their newborn baby and could not come out. Corrie persisted, so he took her to their home where she met the family. He remembered that Corrie held, blessed, and prayed for the new baby. Dr. Richard remembered the year because his son Rajiv was born in 1961.

By the time I heard this story, I felt like I was on holy ground. I thought, *What are the odds that so many coincidences would come together?* I had no idea that Dr. Richard had a connection with New Delhi or Corrie. Still, I wondered what would become of it. There was not much time before my departure. I did not want to get my hopes up and be disappointed.

Dr. Richard distinguished himself even more with me that day. He followed through by contacting the pastor of his old church, and the pastor had responded with a "yes." Even though India was on the other side of the world, the plans had been made in a matter of hours. How rare! Later, I learned that Delhi Bible Fellowship was less than two miles from the hotel where Rob was already staying. Dr. Richard must have known that when he called our meeting "God's providential circumstances."

How easy it was to see God's leading and protection, but how quickly I could forget it too! My luggage did not arrive on the flight with me. In fact, I barely had time to make the quick connection in Toronto. I had survived the sixteen-hour flight from Toronto to India that day, but not without getting swollen ankles and feeling miserable.

I was delayed inside the airport filing a bag claim. My husband was waiting for me outside, without the benefit of knowing what was holding me up. I had no way to contact him, and my stomach was in a knot. When I caught sight of his face, I could see that he was a bit green and had lost weight. He needed the medicine I brought for the "bug" he picked up.

I was exhausted, and my clothes were in the bag that was lost. I was glad that Rob and I were together, but wondered how he had survived for two weeks by himself. I did not always feel God's presence, but still I knew he was there, and I had to trust.

Dr. Richard had also made other contacts for me. He asked one of his friends to take me shopping and be my escort in India. It was a kindness I immediately appreciated. My gratitude of his thoughtfulness grew, as I realized what a difference it made in my visit to India. Pat Samuelson was a gracious hostess to me. She came with her driver to pick me up, and took me shopping in places I could never have gone on my own. She also gave me two additional opportunities to speak to women.

It was a rough start in India, but Pat went out of her way to make sure I had a good week. She introduced me to Pastor Jeremy Dawson at Delhi Bible Fellowship where I was to perform. I was surprised he was not an American. His e-mails to me sure sounded American. When I asked if I would have a translator at the service, he replied, "Why? We speak English." We both laughed. He made plans to pick me up Sunday. I learned I would be giving two performances for approximately three-hundred-fifty people.

The Sunday of my performances was my birthday. I felt that coincidence was another little hug from God. Even though I bounced sometimes between joy and despair, God still loved me and delighted me with his concern for small details.

I had my Corrie costume on when Pastor Jeremy picked Rob and me up on September 12, 2004, to drive us to the church that was in a business area within a mile or two of our hotel. Rob brought his camera, and took the first picture of me as Corrie by the plaque on the outside of the brownstone building.

The pastor took us to the auditorium, and explained that if I stood in the center of the platform and did not move around a lot, everyone sitting in the balcony would be able to see me. The balcony was on the floor above this floor and a space was opened up in the ceiling/floor that allowed rows of benches to be placed so the crowd could see and hear the service. I was equipped with a lapel microphone, and took my seat on the front bench beside Rob. The place began to fill up with a crowd of faces, young and old, from all shades of brown to white.

The worship service was begun by Pastor Sandeep Samuel, and the words to the choruses and hymns were displayed on a large screen. It was as familiar to Rob and me as if it had been in a contemporary church service in Dallas. I immediately teared up as the music touched my heart. I praised God for such an above-and-beyond-what-I-could-imagine opportunity to minister my *Corrie* to God's children on the other side of world. I struggled to control my emotions, so I would be a clear channel of blessing for my talk that was the day's sermon.

After each service I stood by the door to greet the congregation with a, "God bless you!" in my Corrie voice. I save and treasure the responses I heard. One of the sweetest exchanges was from a young man that spoke with love, "Thank you, Mother." "Mother" sounded to me like it was his highest and most honorable title for an older woman. Rob stood out of the way and took photos. I marveled at the grace of God to use me in India. It took my mind off how uncomfortably hot I was in my costume in the New Delhi heat.

The congregation gathered for small, hot cups of chai outside in the area between the church and the building next door. One elderly man approached me to say, "I saw you years ago, but I never thought I'd see you again. But I almost couldn't recognize you because you've lost weight." I looked into his sweet eyes and realized he was dead serious. I thought, *Oh no, he's talking to Corrie.* I did not feel like I could explain, so I agreed with him. I went straight to the pastor to confess, and he assured me he had and would let everyone know that the real Corrie had passed away. That elderly man gave me my highest compliment.

The church in India was surprising in many ways. I did not expect the people there to understand my English better than I could understand them. I had no idea how I would feel "at home with the family of God" there. I may have forgotten some of the things said or done on my India journey, but that feeling remained. Father ten Boom called that feeling a "foretaste of heaven." That feeling was my treasured souvenir of my trip.

Mentor Fred Smith has a term he uses to describe seemingly chance meetings and circumstances. He calls it "beyond arithmetic." I met Dr. Richard at the "Fred in the Bed" session (www.BreakfastwithFred.com) six days before my departure to India. I had no idea that Dr. Richard had lived in New Delhi and had connections there. Those connections were beyond anything I could have arranged even if I tried. I just showed up and God had the plans in place. Performing and teaching in New Delhi was a further expanding of my call to "Go" and I just needed to be willing.

*Dr. John Richard with Corrie ten Boom
in India in 1961.*

The Weaving

Wings to Fly

Corrie became famous for her story of forgiveness. She told about an experience after the war encountering one of the cruelest of her Nazi guards. He asked for her forgiveness, and she knew she was required as a Christian to give it. Corrie recognized her inability to forgive. She confessed her hatred for the man who had beaten her and her sister:

> There was hatred in my heart, but I remembered Romans 5:5. Already we have the love of God shed abroad in our heart. I asked God, *Give me the love to forgive this man.* It was like electricity that came through my arm as I shook his hand and told him, "Brother, I forgive you everything."

Corrie never took credit for her ability to forgive. Instead she would say "Is that Corrie ten Boom love? No, that's God's love!" She quoted a poem of John Bunyon:

Run John, run, The Law commands,
But gives you neither feet nor hands,
Far better news the Gospel brings,
It bids you fly but gives you wings.

Afterwards, Corrie would say, "Isn't that good? God gives you the love he demands of you!"

I had an experience years ago when I needed the love to forgive. I had my own experience of "wings to fly." God gives us impossible assignments, "bids us fly," and then provides the strength to do it. That really is good news!

To me forgiveness is where the rubber hits the road. It is not mouthing my Christian beliefs that is difficult. It is doing them. It just goes against my natural grain to allow injustice to slide. I want to settle the score, and I seem to have my own clear vision of who is wrong and who is right. It is very clear to me in the Bible that God demands that I forgive instead.

Not long after my night of surrender to Christ my pastor told me, "You seem bitter." I immediately dismissed his suggestion with my response, "Oh no, not me." I could have pointed to other people in my life who were bitter, but I sure did not think I was bitter. However, I could not get his words out of my mind. Something inside me suggested that I consider the possibility. I wanted to defend myself. My thoughts raged, *Well, if you just knew what I have to put up with and how I have been treated, you'd see who has the problem. It's them, not me.* That was exactly my point of view, and I probably could have convinced more than a few other people to see it my way.

My pastor's words haunted me that week. *How dare he! The nerve of him to suggest I have a problem!* Still, I knew there were three simple words in my Bible, "Forgive one another." I thought, *Haven't I forgiven tons of people?* It was the few repeat, continual offenders that kept coming to my mind.

As a believer, I knew without a doubt that I was a child of God. I knew that being a Christian was not all about warm hugs from God, but also about obedience. I prayed regularly that he would give me eyes to see and ears to hear him. This particular week he answered me by allowing me to see that I was bitter, and forgiveness was the answer. I also realized that it was not just a hard thing to do, but in these cases it seemed impossible.

I remember the evening I got into bed with my Bible, determined to forgive. I had to get a release from the repeat offenders. I was bitter because I was holding on to how I was hurt. I wrestled nearly all night with the issue. I poured my heart out to God in prayer. *I don't want to be bitter. I know I must forgive. I won't have the forgiveness I need, if I don't. I won't have the peace I crave, if I don't. I WANT to do it. I've tried to do it. I can't do it. Help!*

I did not know how many ways I cried to God. I just knew that I would never forget that night of praying because he heard me. I cried. I mourned. I was miserable. But I meant business and so did he. I did not know how he did it, but he helped me. He allowed the transformation to occur, and my heart was free. I got up the next day knowing God helped me do something I could not accomplish by myself.

Often at my performances, I hear people marveling about Corrie's forgiveness. I hope and pray that they look beyond Corrie to God. My friend Gwen Lam told me about a conversation she had with a woman after my performance at her church in Denton, Texas. Gwen said that the young woman was moved by Corrie's forgiveness, but had decided, "I just couldn't do that." Gwen quickly replied, "That's just the point! Corrie couldn't either. God did it."

The memory of my miserable long night of prayer in 1984 was sweetened by the joy of what I learned. I was glad I chose to obey so I could experience God's help. I am convinced that my growth as a Christian would have stopped if I had refused.

In the classic daily devotional *My Utmost for His Highest*, Oswald Chambers wrote on May 5:

> If Jesus ever gave us a command He could not enable us to fulfill, He would be a liar; and if we make our inability a barrier to obedience, it means we are telling God there is something He has not taken into account. Every element of self-reliance must be slain by the power of God. Complete weakness and dependence will always be the occasion for the Spirit of God to manifest His power.

On December 1 Chambers wrote:

> When we choose deliberately to obey Him, then He will tax the remotest star and the last grain of sand to assist us with all His almighty power.

In my mind, these devotions describe the encouragement of "wings to fly."

Obedience was the key and I knew for sure that I was dependent on God for every breath, and surely for forgiveness. He is able to do the impossible. After I *really* understood that God could do anything, I was never the same. I learned that from my night of forgiveness. God gave my earthbound self "wings to fly" just as he did for Corrie years ago.

Trust and Obey

I waited patiently for the Lord:
And He inclined to me,
And heard my cry.
He also brought me up out of a horrible pit,
Out of the miry clay,
And set my feet upon a rock,
And established my steps.
He has put a new song in my mouth—
Praise to our God;
Many will see it and fear,
And will trust in the Lord.

Psalm 40:1-3 NKJ

In my Bible alongside the verses above I have written, "This is the story of my life." God rescued me and put a new song in my heart.

I am intrigued by the place suffering has played in my life. Thornton Wilder wrote some lines in his play *The Angel that Troubled the Water* which spoke to me about my life:

> Without your wounds, where would your power be? It is your very remorse that makes your low voice tremble into the heart of men. The very angels themselves could not persuade the wretched and blundering children on earth as can one human being broken on the wheels of living. In Love's service only the wounded soldiers can serve.

God used the suffering in Corrie's life to allow her the opportunities to speak to the world. As Betsie told her in prison, "They will believe us because we have been *here*!" That conviction inspired me to tell my story because maybe where I have been will help someone else. I like the saying that God will never waste a hurt. He hurts us as little as possible to make us into vessels he can use.

God gives us the strength we need even in our suffering. Corrie wrote about a train ticket lesson from her father. When she was a child, Corrie worried she would not be strong enough to suffer for Christ. Father explained that when they traveled together on the train, he did not give her the ticket ahead of time. She received it just in time to get on the train. Father reassured Corrie that when she needed the strength, God would give her the ticket just in time.

Corrie had to trust and I have to trust. I am commanded:

> *Trust in the Lord with all your heart and lean not on your own understanding. In all your ways, acknowledge him and he will direct your path.* Proverbs, 3:5-6 NKJ

Sometimes I find myself looking up to heaven with a "What's this all about?" attitude written all over my face. I read about an expression that Corrie used, "I'll just put that on a hook." She used that when the situation did not make sense, but she trusted that someday she might be able to see God's purposes in the situation. I have to learn to trust completely.

One of my favorite artists, Thomas Hart Benton, taught that the artist has to start with the "Grand Design." The details to the grand design are filled in as the artist works. That reminds me of a verse of scripture:

> *For we are His workmanship, created in Christ Jesus for good works, which God prepared beforehand that we should walk in them.* Ephesians 2:10 NIV.

I must believe that God has my "Grand Design" figured out and plans for me.

I read a verse in The Message Bible with new eyes:

> *If people can't see what God is doing, they stumble all over themselves; but when they attend to what he reveals, they are most blessed.* Proverbs 29:18

It jumped out at me that I have often stumbled because I just could not see what God was up to in my life. Much of what I have written in this book, I have only been able to see by looking back. I could not always see the plan when I was in the middle of it. I had to trust.

The second part of the verse is about attending to what God reveals—obedience. Dr. Dorothy Patterson of Southwestern Baptist

Theological Seminary told me about her interview with the actress Jeanette Clift George who spent time with Corrie and played her in the movie *The Hiding Place*. Dr. Patterson asked Jeanette for one word to describe Corrie. Without hesitation, she replied, "Obedience."

Father gave Corrie a memorable lesson on obedience when she was a child. She did not want to go to school. She fought Father's efforts to take her from the porch by holding tightly to the railing. She told about how much her fingers hurt when Father pried them loose and took her anyway. She told that story to remind us to obey and not hold too tightly to the things of the world, because it hurts if God has to pry our fingers loose from whatever we are holding on to.

I have often sung to myself the lyrics to the familiar hymn "Trust and Obey" below:

> *Trust and obey*
> *For there's no other way*
> *To be happy in Jesus*
> *But to trust and obey.*

I want to be happy in Jesus and there is *no other way*. I had to tell myself that meant me and that meant now. It is not trust and *understand*, it is trust and *obey*. I have studied Corrie's life now for more than twenty years. She learned to trust God when she was a child, and she learned to obey. I realized that she could not always see what her next step would be anymore than I could. All life boils down to simply trusting and obeying—no matter who you are.

Corrie's Glove Lesson

From *Corrie ten Boom Live*:

I have here a glove. What can the glove do? It can do nothing. But when my hand is in the glove, it can do many things…it can cook, it can write, it can even play the piano. Well you say, that's not the glove that does it, that is the hand in the glove. That is so. I tell you we are nothing but gloves. The hand in the glove is the Holy Spirit of God. We cannot do anything if we are only near the glove, we must be filled. I say to you, "Be filled with the Spirit so you can do the work he has planned for you!"

Corrie would say that the happiest commandment to obey is "Be filled with the Spirit." The glove visual aid is an encouragement to me about the issue of obedience. I have the power to obey, when I am filled with the Spirit. When I am afraid or when the job of obeying is impossible, I remember Corrie's glove lesson. I pray to be filled with the Spirit, and then I'll have what it takes to accomplish what I have been put on earth to do. God has the design in place, and he is weaving his plans for me *and* for you.

80th Birthday Celebration: Dennis Cleaver, Evelyn, Susan Pritchard, Marie Cleaver, Margaret Peed, Leah Beth Nelson, Joyce Newbury, and Alan Cleaver

Evelyn with Gigi Graham

Rob, Evelyn, Gloria Jones, Charlie "Tremendous" Jones (2005 Award Recipient), John Wesley Czarnota at Roaring Lambs Hall of Fame Banquet

Marie Cleaver at age 82:
There is nothing so beautiful as
peace and joy in an old face!

Endorsements

"*Being privileged to know Evelyn Hinds personally makes her reenactment of Corrie ten Boom's life even more fascinating for me. She makes me laugh, cry, angry, reflective, and appreciative of this remarkable woman, all in the span of 45 minutes. Her stage presence, heavily accented voice, body language, and facial expressions, as she acts out portions of Corrie's life, is all first class. Her entire purpose is to highlight the influence faith in God can have in one person's life— one who never wavers as she spreads it to all she touches. Evelyn has a wonderful gift that she freely shares with others through the stage. Now she has put it in a book that we all need to read more than once.*"

Vernon B. Lewis, Jr.
Major General, U.S. Army Ret.

"*Evelyn skillfully weaves her story along with the venerable Corrie ten Boom's in this remarkable book. Her compassion for those who are wounded and her desire to share what Christ did in her life, and can do for them, make for a powerful read.*"

Susie Hawkins
Bible Study Teacher

"*Evelyn Hinds is a talented actress. She is also an equally talented author. She has studied and portrayed Corrie ten Boom and now she has given us an opportunity to look at her and Corrie in a new and exciting way. You will be spiritually lifted after reading this fine piece of writing.*"

Garry D. Kinder
Businessman and Bible Teacher

For more information or additional copies,
contact Evelyn Hinds at:

Arts Touching Hearts, Inc.
P.O. Box 631714
Irving, TX 75063-1714
972. 401.8907
evelyn@evelynhinds.com

Or visit www.evelynhinds.com or
www.corrietenboomlive.com

www.CornerStoneLeadership.com